JAMES II

ENGLISH MONARCHS   TREASURES FROM THE NATIONAL ARCHIVES

JAMES II

The triumph
and the tragedy

JOHN CALLOW

THE NATIONAL ARCHIVES

First published in 2005 by

The National Archives
Kew, Richmond
Surrey TW9 4DU
UK

www.nationalarchives.gov.uk/

The National Archives (TNA) was formed when the Public Record Office and Historical
Manuscripts Commission (HMC) combined in April 2003

A catalogue record for this book is available from the British Library

ISBN 1 903365 57 0

Designed by Penny Jones and Michael Morris, Brentford, Middlesex

Printed and bound in Malta on behalf of Compass Press Ltd

ILLUSTRATIONS

Cover: James II by John Riley, c.1690. Facing the greatest military and political challenges of
his career, James unsurprisingly chose to present a grim and uncompromising figure: setting his
jaw firmly, as he regarded the artist in his place of refuge in Dublin Castle. Background: A letter
from James to Prince William of Orange (see Document 8). Pamphlet: The Address of the Lords
Spiritual and Temporal and Commons Assembled at Westminster, London, 1689. With James
fled to France, and rebellion threatening in Ireland, the hastily assembled Convention Parliament
sought to entrust Prince William with the full powers of the executive.

Half-title: A detail of James in Classical dress, as Lord High Admiral, by Henri Gascars, 1672–73.

Frontispiece: James as a victorious general, by Sir Peter Lely, c.1664–65. Though the suit
of full-plate armour bears no relation to anything that the Duke would have actually worn on the
battlefield, it – together with the baton of command held firmly in his grip – instantly conveys
to the viewer a vision of James's military prowess and his desire to resume his career as a
soldier in the coming war against the Dutch. Note the signet ring, on his little finger, with which
he stamped all of his correspondence.

Title page: The Great Seal of King James II. This was used to certify all the acts of government
and aimed to reflect the power and apparent unchangeability of the monarchical system. Thus,
the image of the sovereign did not necessarily alter with the change of ruler. Compare this with
the seal of Charles II on page 44.

Contents page: James at his religious devotions, in 1694, from a print that was once owned
by Samuel Pepys.

Page xii (facing Preface): This contemporary engraving shows James in his ceremonial robes
as a Knight of the Order of the Garter. His arms as Duke of York are prominently displayed,
emphasising his royal birth and place in the succession. The recreation of the Order, in 1660,
served to further underline the resurgence of the monarchy.

Contents

Acknowledgements

I am particularly grateful to Jane Crompton for her trust and guidance in helping to prepare this book, and for commissioning it in the first place, together with my very first published work. I would also like to thank the staff of the British Library, and in particular the Department of Rare Books, for their unfailing help and unflagging good humour; and Professor Jeffrey Richards for his help, constancy and good counsel. I am particularly indebted to Miss Pamela Clark, the Registrar of the Royal Archives at Windsor, for making King James's original memoirs available to me, and for all her help and kind assistance while I was researching there.

This book is for Shen and Tom, as a testament to friendship.

A Note on Dating

While many European nations had adopted the Gregorian (or New Style) Calendar over the course of the seventeenth century, Great Britain and Ireland were to remain stubbornly loyal to the Julian (or Old Style) Calendar until 1752. The result was that the British and Irish calendars lagged behind that which was generally used across the rest of Western Europe. In 1700 this difference was to increase to eleven days. Naturally this causes difficulties for the historian in attempting to provide a coherent overview of events on both sides of the Channel. For the sake of clarity, all the dates used in the text are given in the Old Style, unless the actions recorded occurred after 1752. For events on the Continent, both Old and New Style dates are given. As in modern usage, the New Year is taken as beginning on 1 January and not on 25 March.

Series Note

Most of the key historic documents selected for this series are from the collections at The National Archives; a few are reproduced courtesy of other important national or private repositories.

Each key document is reproduced on a numbered double-page spread with an explanatory introduction placing it in context. (Selected pages or details have been chosen for lengthy items.) Transcripts, with modernized spellings and explanations of archaic words, are provided where necessary. All the documents featured on these spreads are cross-referenced in the main text.

If you would like to see the original documents at The National Archives at Kew, please see www.nationalarchives.gov.uk or phone 020 8392 5200 for information about how to obtain a free Reader's Ticket.

For further information about titles in the ENGLISH MONARCHS series or other publications from The National Archives, please send your name and address to:

Publications Marketing, The National Archives, FREEPOST SEA 7565, Richmond, Surrey, UK TW9 4DU (stamp required from overseas)

To order any publication from The National Archives, visit www.nationalarchives.gov.uk/bookshop/

All titles 128 pages and priced at £14.99

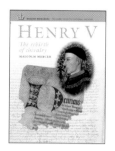

Henry V

The Rebirth of Chivalry

Malcolm Mercer

ISBN: 1 903365 71 6

Richard III

A Royal Enigma

Sean Cunningham

ISBN: 1 903365 45 7

Elizabeth I

The Golden Reign of Gloriana

David Loades

ISBN: 1 903365 43 0

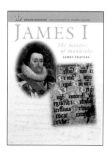

James I

The Masque of Monarchy

James Travers

ISBN: 1 903365 56 2

The Documents

His Royall Highness Iames Duke of Yorke and Albany
K.t of the most noble order of the Garter, and sole
brother to his sacred Ma.ty King Charles the 2.d &c.a

Preface

The life of James II was shaped in equal measure by war, revolution and bitter religious conflict. As a youth he knew the exhilaration of battle but also tasted the bitterness of defeat. During the Restoration, he left his stamp upon almost every department of the Early Modern State. He was just as at home in the board rooms of the City of London, discussing schemes for trade and empire, as he was poring over plans for new designs at the Navy Office, or chairing the meetings of the Scottish Privy Council in Edinburgh. Although his open profession of Roman Catholicism effectively destabilised English politics for a generation, he ascended the throne on a wave of popular support. He then succeeded in quickly consolidating his hold on office, easily defeating two rebellions and launching an unprecedented growth in the power of the executive and the strength of the military. Yet within less than three years he had lost his crown and found himself a hunted fugitive, roughly manhandled by a group of sailors in a small village on the Kentish coast. While he considered himself an authority upon navigation, was a founding member of the Royal Society, and impressed Louis XIV's scientists and astronomers, this most difficult and troubled of kings was to die in exile in the style of a humble penitent, desperate to make atonement for his sins. Unable to brook dissent, or to heed timely advice, James's utter inflexibility of character and steely purpose turned all of his many gifts and advantages to dust, effectively retarding the cause of full religious toleration by one hundred and fifty years and bequeathing to Jacobitism – the movement that bore his name – an untenable commitment to French power and to a centralising form of Roman Catholic kingship. His tragedy was essentially that of a man promoted far beyond his abilities, or understanding, who never flinched from confronting head-on the most intractable religious and political problems of a turbulent age, and who presided over both the growth and the collapse of plans for an absolute monarchy in Great Britain. His failures, just as surely as his triumphs, are written into every civil liberty and political freedom that we enjoy today.

The Warrior Prince

CHILDHOOD AND CIVIL WAR

From the outset it had not been an easy pregnancy. The Queen, Henrietta Maria, had fallen while out walking with her friends and had been ordered to confine herself to bed immediately by her loving and concerned husband, King Charles I. However, despite the fears of the attendant physicians, who had expected and prepared for the worst, she proved strong enough to thoroughly confound medical opinion by giving birth to 'a goodly, lusty' baby boy, on the night of 14 October 1633, at St James's Palace. Her fourth child and second surviving son was quickly accorded the titles of Duke of York and Albany, and named in honour of his grandfather – James I of England and VI of Scotland – who had, a generation earlier, successfully united the English and Scottish crowns. Spontaneous popular celebrations and officially sanctioned events accompanied his sumptuous and costly baptism (see Document 1, *A royal christening*). After the last bonfire was finally extinguished and the child's christening gifts were carefully packed away, the little Prince was returned, once more, to the safety of his nursery and largely disappeared from public sight.

Brought up alongside his elder brother, Charles, the Prince of Wales, at a special 'children's' court at Richmond in Surrey, James learned to read and write adequately enough, and to memorise the Anglican catechism, under the supervision of a succession of worthy, if rather uninspiring, tutors. The young Prince was a lively and adventurous child, who 'cared not to plod upon his games; for his active soul was more delighted with quick and nimble recre-ations, as running, leaping [and] riding'. Untroubled by arduous

A self-assured and flamboyant Charles I surrounded by the trappings of monarchy, before the disasters of civil war had overtaken him and wrecked both his peoples and kingdoms. Painted by Daniel Mytens (1633). For eleven years, between 1629 and 1640, he had chosen to rule without Parliament, fashioning about him an elaborate court culture and the belief that the king was God's representative upon earth. His disastrous attempt to transform the established church and to impose a new form of worship upon his Scots subjects led to the collapse of his personal government and the fateful decision to recall MPs to Westminster.

A royal christening

The order of ceremony for James's baptism in November 1633, as prepared by an anonymous royal servant.

James's christening on 24 November 1633 represented the first public event of his life and was therefore an occasion which necessitated careful planning. New galleries and scaffolds were built in the chapel of St James's Palace to house spectators and musicians, while cloths of gold were hung from the walls and rich carpets laid underfoot. Even though he had no way of knowing it at the time, the circumstances surrounding his baptism reflected, in microcosm, many of the doctrinal conflicts that were to shape James's entire adult life. His witnesses, as his godparents were known, were Elizabeth the 'Winter Queen' of Bohemia and Frederick Henry, Prince of Orange, who held impeccable Protestant credentials, but neither was able to attend, so deputies were appointed to act in their stead. In their absence, the focus of attention shifted to Archbishop Laud, whose redecoration of the chapel, positioning of the altar table and costly vestments spoke louder than any words of his intent to implement a thorough-going change in both the liturgy and religious practices of the established Church.

While Charles I looked on from a window above, and the Queen absented herself from the proceedings, Laud took the baby in his arms, anointing him with water from the silver basin, held by the Earl of Hertford, and named the child in honour of his grandfather, King James VI of Scotland and I of England. He then listed his titles as Duke of York and Albany, symbolising the union of the English and Scottish Crowns, while music was struck up and the courtiers and aldermen shouted out their greetings to the wriggling infant. Only the Lord Mayor's gift of a 'fair bowl' filled to the brim with coins struck an awkward note, as it was discovered upon closer inspection that it was made of silver, rather than gold as had been originally thought.

Despite this, the occasion was judged to have been a great success, with instructions sent in advance to the warships on the Thames, to the Governor of the Tower of London and to the Heralds, who were to conduct the assembled lords and ladies to their places in the chapel. In a rigidly hierarchical age, when symbolism and questions of privilege and place were of the utmost importance, nothing could be left to chance. As a result, the ceremony was carefully scripted by a royal servant several days before the actual ceremony in November 1633.

THE DOCUMENT READS:

The warning being given, the trumpets sound and drums beaten and the signals are put up to give notice to the Tower and our ships for discharging of the ordinance. Then the Duke with his attendants is brought to the Altar, the officers of Arms going before him, which the Lord [Treasurer] offereth for him, the Duke, or some other appointed for him.
Being returned, Clarencieux [the King at Arms] conducts the Godfather up to the offering, and after that Norry [the King at Arms] conducts the Godmother in like manner. The offering done and service ended, they return as they came, saving the Lord that carried the basin, takes his place according to his degree.

Then warning being giuen the Trumpets
sound and Drums beate. and the Signalls
are put vp to giue notice to the Forts
& Ships for dischargᵍ of the Ordnance.
Then the Duke with his attendants is brought
out of his Trauiss and conducted to the Altar
the officers of Armes going before him,
where the L: Priest offereth for him
the Duke. or some other appointed for
him.
Being returned, Clarencieux conducts the
Godfathers up to the Offering
And after that Norroy conducts the
Godmother in like manner.
The Offering done & seruice ended
they returne as they came sauing the Lord
that carried the Bason: takes his place
according to his degree.

56

An altogether more sombre Charles I, scarred and disillusioned by the experience of war, accepts a pen from James, as storm clouds gather and block out the sun. Painted by Lely in 1647, when both father and son were the prisoners of Parliament at Hampton Court, this work well conveys the sense of duty to the Royalist cause burned into the boy by defeat and personal humiliation.

academic demands and permitted to explore his own sporting interests, in archery, fencing and hunting, James's strength and sheer physicality quickly signalled his aptitude for a military career.

Already the storm clouds of civil war had begun to gather about Great Britain and Ireland, as Charles I's largely divisive innovations in Church and State were effectively challenged in each of his three kingdoms. With full-scale rebellions raging across Scotland and Ireland, James's carefree and pampered existence came to an abrupt end as his father attempted to call, and then to curtail, the business of two parliaments in quick succession. After he tried to mount a pre-emptive strike against the leaders of the opposition, which failed in January 1642, the City's Trained Bands were turned out against the King, and Charles I was forced to flee his capital.

Amid the initial confusion, as both King and Parliament attempted to raise armies and to stockpile arms, James appears to have been forgotten. He was only sent for by his father several weeks later, in March 1642. Fortunately, although orders had already been issued by Parliament for his detention, the Prince's elderly governor – the Marquis of Hertford – chose to disobey them and to answer the royal summons instead, hurrying north with the boy to join the King at York. James's safe arrival was the cause of wild celebrations, and he was invested with the Order of the Garter by his proud father. However, within a matter of weeks the uncertainty of the times and Charles I's willingness to use his son as an instrument of policy would combine to place James in even greater peril.

During the wars against the Scots, the port of Hull had served as an enormous supply depot, and the King was not slow in realising its potential value for equipping a new army. Intending to allay the fears of the Governor, Sir John Hotham, whose loyalty was in doubt, he sent James on ahead into the city, to prepare for his coming. Unfortunately, the next morning, when the King let it be known that he wished to take possession of the place, the Governor raised the drawbridges, barred the city gates, and ordered the garrison to stand to, ready for action. Try as he might, Charles I could not persuade the Governor and, more importantly, his soldiers to yield the stronghold to his authority. After a tense stand-off, he broke camp and set off back to Beverley, having negotiated no more than the release of his son and his escort. Having spent the best part of a day in captivity, and seen his father publicly humbled, James bridled at the indignity and, significantly, drew his own conclusions from the incident. The King and his men had failed through their weakness in wishing to negotiate. Had they used force, or seized Hotham at the first opportunity, then, he believed, things would have gone very differently and both city and arsenal would have been successfully taken.

This romantic Victorian painting by Henry Dawson recreates the moment, on 22 August 1642, when Charles I raised his standard at Nottingham, and effectively declared war against his own subjects. Strong winds later blew down the banner, in the night, which was seen as a bad omen for his fortunes in the war.

For the remainder of the spring, and throughout the summer months, James followed in the wake of his father and the embryonic Royalist army, scouring Yorkshire, the Welsh Borders and the Midlands in search of fresh recruits and weapons, to make good those denied to them at Hull. He saw the Royal Standard unfurled at Nottingham Castle, signalling the formal commencement of hostilities, and – just days after his ninth birthday – witnessed the opening battle of the English Civil Wars, from the slopes of Edgehill (see Document 2, *The Battle of Edgehill*, for his own account). With the fighting proving indecisive and the advance of the Royalist army upon London stalling at Turnham Green, the King chose Oxford as his new capital.

It was there among the spires and university colleges that James spent most of the next three and a half years. However, rather than being a seat of learning, the city now resembled a principal theatre of the war, with the college greens resounding to the noise of troops being drilled. The young Prince heard exciting tales of the latest cavalry raids and infantry skirmishes from officers returning from campaign. Moreover, through his daily contact with those of

A proud, if a little wary, James sat for this portrait by William Dobson, in wartime Oxford. When the city fell, the canvas was left unfinished.

James's own eyewitness account, transcribed by a clerk in Mary of Modena's household.

After blundering after one another across the Warwickshire countryside for six days, the Royalist and Parliamentary armies collided on the slopes of Edgehill on 23 October 1642. As a nine-year-old boy, James watched the unfolding action from the heights at the rear of the Royalist position and only narrowly avoided capture as a party of enemy troopers slipped round their flank. The King's horse had met with early success and swept the majority of the Parliamentary cavalry from the field, but they had failed to capitalise upon their advantage by rallying in time to come to the assistance of their foot. In their absence, the advance of the Royalist infantry was checked and the fight rapidly degenerated into a bloody stalemate. By nightfall, contrary to all expectations, nothing had been decided and some 3,000 Englishmen lay dead or wounded as the frost formed upon the ground.

Years later James recorded this traumatic boyhood experience and, at the beginning of the eighteenth century, Etienne Dumirail transcribed his notes, on the orders of Mary of Modena, to form the text of the King's official autobiography. This rich and graphic account was printed in 1816 and forms the principal source for James's life. Revealing his deep sense of patriotism, James recalled the shock, noise and carnage of his first battle.

THE TEXT READS:

His Majesty with the Prince of Wales and the Duke of York, marched immediately after the foot, attended by several of the Lords whom he had commanded to stay by him, and by the band of [Gentlemen] pensioners on horseback led on by their Lieutenant, Sir William Howard, and that it might be known in what part of the Army the person of the King was, he had a scarlet cornet larger than ordinary carried before him. When the Royal Army was advanced within musket shot of the enemy, the foot on both sides began to fire, the King's [infantry] still coming on, and the rebels' continuing only to keep their ground; so that they came so near to one another …

The text continues in the illustrated page:

that some of the battalions were at push of pike, particularly the regiment of Guards commanded by the Lord Willoughby and the General's regiment, with some others; in so much that the Lord Willoughby with his pike killed an officer of the Earl of Essex's own regiment, and hurt another. The foot being thus engaged in such warm and close service, it were reasonable to imagine that one side should run and be disordered; but it happened otherwise, for each as if by mutual consent retired some few paces, and then stuck down their colours, continuing to fire at one another even till night; a thing so very

The text continues:

extraordinary, that nothing less than so many witnesses as were there present, could make it credible; nor can any other reason be given for it, but the natural courage of English men, which prompted them to maintain their ground, though the rawness and inexperience of both parties had not furnished them with skill to make the best use of their advantages. It is observed that of all nations the English stick closest to their officers, and it is hardly seen that our common soldiers will turn their backs, if they who command them do not first show them the bad example, or leave them un-officered by being killed, themselves, upon the place.

The foot so close to one
another that they are
within push of pike
ibid:

that some of the Batalions were
at push of pike, particularly the
Regiment of Guards commanded
by the Lord Willouby, and the
Generalls Regiment, with some
others; in so much that the Lord
Willouby with his pike kill'd an
Officer of the Earle of Essex his
own Regiment, and hurt another.
The Foot being thus ingaged in
such warm and close service, it
were reasonable to imagine that
one side should run and be
disorderd; but it happen'd otherwise, for each as if by mutuall
consent, retired some few paces, and
then stick down their coulours
continuing to fire at one another
even till night; a thing so very

The Foot continue till
night firing at one
another
Ibid.

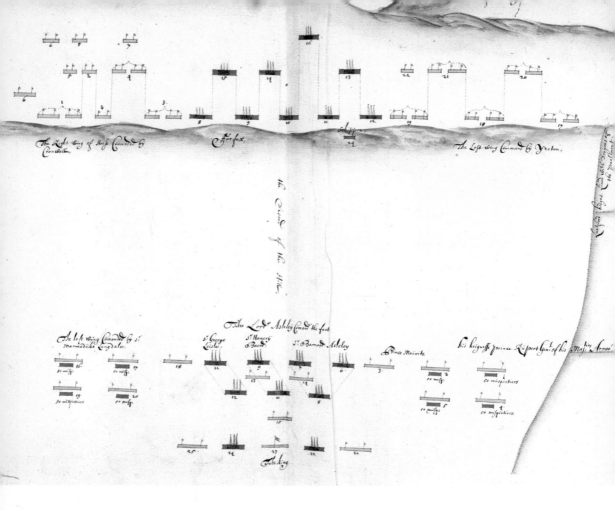

The various labels on the plan include:

The Right Wing of Horse Comanded by Cromwell.
Sr Fairfax
Skippon
The Quarters of the Hill
The Left Wing Comanded by Yreton.

The Left wing Comanded by Sr Marmaduke Langdale.
Sr George Lisle.
Sr Hanery Bacon.
The Lord Astley Comand the foot
Sr Barnard Astley.
Prince Maurits
his heighnesse prince Rupert Genl of his Majs Armes

A contemporary plan of the battle of Naseby, 14 June 1645, showing the position of the Parliamentary (at top) and Royalist (at bottom) forces. Rejecting the advice of his generals, Charles I insisted on forcing the engagement, in an attempt to turn the tide of the war. The result was disaster, and as the King fled the field that afternoon, his army had ceased to exist and his cause lay in tatters.

the King's followers who now crowded into Oxford's tenements, having been displaced by the war, James was exposed to a particularly uncompromising brand of High Anglican, and ultra-Royalist, politics. Indeed, their example of faithful sacrifice and their eventual plight, as the tide of the conflict began to turn against the King, were to do much to shape James's later intolerance of political dissent, and his predisposition to equate even mild criticism with the workings of faction and the practice of treason.

As he was too young to accompany them in the field, James could only listen to the reports of the defeats of the regiments that bore his name. The Duke of York's Horse was badly mauled at Marston Moor, in July 1644, while his regiment of foot was destroyed at

Naseby, in June of the following year. Having lost a high proportion of his officer corps and presided over the annihilation of his veteran infantry, at the latter battle, King Charles was finally forced to acknowledge the possibility of defeat. As food grew short and units of Parliament's New Model Army closed in around Oxford, the King abandoned both the city and his second son to their fate. No provision had been made for the safety of the Duke of York, and James awoke on the morning of 27 April 1646 to find his father gone. He would later recall, with more than a touch of bitterness, that 'the King had it once in his thoughts to have carried the Duke along with him, but did not'.

On 20 June 1646 the city finally surrendered and James found himself the prisoner of Parliament. Separated from his own servants and even the little dwarf of whom he had become particularly fond, he was sent back to London and placed in the custody of the Earl of Northumberland.

Though painted a generation later, Jan Wyck's view of Oxford under siege, provides an excellent idea of both the Royalist fortifications thrown-up to defend the city, and the Parliamentarian entrenchments that ringed it, preventing re-supply and finally sealing its fate.

ESCAPE AND EXILE

Luckily for James, the Earl proved to be a kind and extremely generous governor, who placed few restrictions on his activities and appeared to be highly embarrassed by his position as both the boy's guardian and jailer. With Charles I now also a prisoner of Parliament, and plans afoot to depose him and to set one of his sons in his place, the King sent word to his agents that he would look upon James's escape as his own preservation. Though early attempts failed through the interception of his letters, the Duke was able to establish contact with Colonel Joseph Bampfield and to formulate a plan for his escape in the spring of 1648.

Accordingly, on the night of 21 to 22 April he finished his supper and, as usual, began a game of hide-and-seek with the other children who shared his apartments at St James's Palace. This time, however, he made sure to shut away his younger sister's lap dog, which followed him everywhere he went, and slipped down the backstairs unnoticed. Opening the door with a key that he had borrowed from the gardener that morning, he hurried across the parkland as the snow began to fall. Bampfield was waiting with a coach to carry him across the City to a safe house and on to the Thames-side. James's deception worked perfectly – though there is some reason to suspect that Northumberland may actually have been glad to have him gone – and more than an hour elapsed before the Earl and his servants began to search for him. Even then, all that could be found of him were a few impressions of his footsteps in the fresh snow. Disguised as a young girl, he was able to board a ship before the ports could be sealed off or an effective pursuit mounted.

Though he troubled the sailors by his un-ladylike behaviour and his constant tugging at his uncomfortable stockings during the crossing, James reached the coast of Holland safely. He went at once to the court of his elder sister, Princess Mary, at The Hague, which had become a refuge for Royalist exiles. His troubles, however, were far from over. He was denied active commands

News of the judicial execution of Charles I at Whitehall, on 30 January 1649, created shockwaves across Europe and shook thrones from the Escorial to the Kremlin. In this contemporary German engraving, the King's soul is raised up to heaven while Generals Cromwell and Fairfax are held jointly responsible for the deed.

that he believed to be his by right and was devastated to learn of his father's trial and execution during a visit to his mother in Paris at the beginning of February 1649. Having donned the official black dress of mourning, distinguished only by his jewelled Garter Star, he accompanied his brother, Charles, to the island of Jersey – which was still held by the Royalists – but did not go with him on his subsequent voyage to Scotland; it was well known that James disapproved of his brother's willingness to treat with their former enemies.

A SOLDIER OF FORTUNE

Back in Paris, James lobbied hard to gain the military commission that he so desperately desired. Initially, things went well and a troop of horse was promised to him, but fear of English displeasure at such an appointment and the rebellion of the Prince de Condé, which threatened to pull down the French monarchy, ensured that the position was never given to him. However, James found a new and unexpected ally in one of his brother's leading advisors, Sir Edward Hyde. Hyde suggested a compromise whereby he might still go to the wars, but as a gentleman volunteer rather than as a commissioned officer. It was thus that James, Duke of York, entered French service and rode off for campaign with two companions, all on borrowed horses. His camp bed swayed uneasily behind him, strapped to the back of a reluctant mule.

James received his baptism of fire in May 1652 (New Style) amid a confused and scrappy firefight for control of the suburbs of Étampes. In June he led one of the assault parties that threw Condé's troops back upon the walls of Paris. His reckless bravery and his consummate skill as a horseman quickly brought him to the attention of Marshal Turenne, the commander of the French royal army. A firm friendship grew up between the two men, based upon mutual respect and understanding. Indeed, as the Marshal's eyesight began to fail, James was increasingly employed by him to scout out the enemy positions. Turenne took great pride in James's daring exploits in gathering intelligence and eluding enemy patrols. There was scarcely an aspect of seventeenth-century warfare that he did not experience; under Turenne's careful tutelage, he observed the work of military engineers in opening siege lines and learned to conduct supply convoys through hostile territory.

At Ligny Castle the ice broke under his advancing soldiers. James was lucky to escape the withering fire of the garrison, which cut down four of his captains close about him. At Mousson he worked through the night in a flooded trench, overseeing the laying of a mine underneath the enemy's tower.

The memories of the smoke and fury of battle, the sight of frozen corpses lining the roads in mid-winter, and the rough camaraderie of the soldiers who referred to the cabbage stalks they were forced to eat as 'the Cardinal's bread' would stay with James for the rest of his life. Despite the evident hardships, he viewed his period of service with the French army as a uniquely happy and rewarding time. With Turenne's patronage, promotion came quickly and, after only two years' service, James was promoted to the rank of Lieutenant General in the spring of 1654. Still not quite 21, he proudly noted that, according to the date of his commission, he was the youngest general serving in the campaign.

Sir Edward Hyde, Lord Clarendon, painted in his robes as Lord Chancellor after the Restoration. A statesman of diligence, moderation and the highest intelligence, he was virtually the head of Charles II's government until his fall from power in 1667. No Stuart monarch had a more loyal or capable servant, and both Charles and James would have done better to heed his wise counsel.

Unfortunately, however, his sense of fulfilment was suddenly and quite unexpectedly shattered when the governments of England and France signed a peace treaty, and he was obliged to surrender his command. James tried everything he could to remain at the court in Paris, hoping desperately that his fortunes might once more change for the better. Eventually he was compelled to leave the realm and take service with Condé and the Spanish, his former foes. Aside from the purely personal consequence of having to say a mournful farewell to Turenne and his brother officers, this break in James's military apprenticeship also had far deeper and more long-lasting repercussions for his practice of command. Though he had proved himself a courageous soldier and an able subordinate, he had never tasted a truly independent command. Deprived of Turenne's fatherly advice and guiding genius, the memory of half-

Marshal Turenne portrayed as a Roman General. Though he knew defeat as well as victory, Turenne seldom commanded forces equal or superior to his foes. Yet he wrought wonders with the often-meagre resources afforded to him by his political masters. Intelligent and fearless, he always looked after the welfare of his soldiers and deserves to be remembered as the greatest commander of his age.

learned maxims and past successes would soon ossify, to leave James with an inflexible and increasingly hide-bound approach to warfare that one day would prove to be his undoing.

James soon came into conflict with the Spanish generals. He believed them to be dilatory and overly concerned with unnecessary formalities, instead of prosecuting the war to the best of their abilities. He was frustrated by their premature decision to call off an attack upon a fort that guarded the approach to Mardyck which he felt stood every chance of success. Later he joined with Condé in voicing his disquiet as the Spanish army, sent to relieve Dunkirk, found itself outmanoeuvred and forced to fight an Anglo-French force under the command of Marshal Turenne among the sand dunes outside the town.

With both the battle and the key seaport of Dunkirk lost (see Document 3, *The sale of Dunkirk*), the Spanish army prepared to go into winter quarters. Meanwhile, James found, to his surprise, that even the news of the death of Oliver Cromwell did little to alleviate his situation. With the hoped-for Royalist uprisings either failing to materialise or being speedily crushed, Republican government in England appeared to be worryingly durable. So James resigned himself to accepting a command as High Admiral of Spain in the war against the Portuguese. Then suddenly the competing factions and crippling debts under which the English Republic had laboured threatened to tear it apart from the inside. General Monck led his regiments south in order to restore order and to open covert negotiations aimed at bringing Charles Stuart back across the Channel as a king. James could hardly believe the pace of events, nor the 'wonderful changes, which were almost daily produced in England'. He noted that 'when the motion was once begun, it went on so fast' that both he and Charles II were back in their 'own country, before those abroad, [and] especially the Spaniards, would believe there was any revolution towards it'.

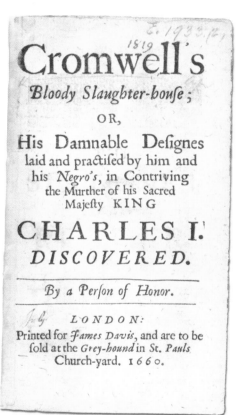

The reputations of military hard-men often undergo rapid reversals. The print on the left, from 1651, shows Oliver Cromwell as a victorious general at the height of his powers. The pamphlet on the right, produced by John Gauden during the political reaction of 1660, demonises him and dehumanises his republican followers. They are reduced to the level of the black African slaves, who were soon to be shipped, at James's behest, to the New World.

A letter from James to Marshal Turenne, commander of the French royal army, 13 September 1662.

At the Battle of the Dunes, on 14/24 June 1658, James controlled the centre of the Spanish army but, from the first, things went badly. A charge by the Cromwellian regiments buckled his line and the French artillery, supported by the guns of English ships anchored along the coast, tore great holes in the massed ranks of Spanish pikemen. It was with the greatest difficulty that James was able to stem the tide of the attack by leading repeated cavalry charges and bringing up fresh reinforcements from the rear. However, it was too little too late. The flanks of the Spanish army were staved in by the French, and English battle standards were, at last, planted in triumph upon the top of the central dunes. As his troops disintegrated, James narrowly escaped capture and rode through the shattered remnants of the Spanish camp to rejoin the main body of fugitives, as they regrouped further along the coast.

For the next four years Dunkirk belonged to England, but by 1662 the restored monarchy of Charles II was already experiencing an acute financial crisis. In order to raise funds quickly, it was decided by Charles II, in conjunction with Clarendon, that the port should be sold back to France, regardless of its enormous strategic value. Due to his good contacts at the French court and his continuing friendship with Marshal Turenne, James was used as an intermediary to speed up the pace of the negotiations. Consequently, despite widespread opposition, Dunkirk was sold to Louis XIV for the sum of five million livres in October 1662. Though well below the original asking price, James seems to have been well pleased with the deal and had been instrumental in its successful conclusion.

On 13 September 1662 James wrote to Turenne about Dunkirk and his hopes for resuming his military career.

THE LETTER READS:

I couldn't help writing to you because of the desire I have, that the matter of Dunkirk should be resolved, obliged me to seek from the Chancellor [Clarendon] all the possible ways imaginable to achieve this, and since he brings as much enthusiasm as I do to it, the only thing holding us up is to calculate how much money the King my brother will take for it.

In the light of the state of affairs, we cannot find any other expedient, than to give valid assurances to London, until the amount is negotiated, to remedy the present state of affairs, during the time the King promised.

I can assure you, that apart from this pressing necessity, the King my brother will accept all the conditions which the King of France has desired.

His strongest held concern, mine, and that of the Chancellor is to form a close friendship [with Louis XIV] and to link our interests with his, so that I am certain that you will make the correct judgement. Because of the King my brother's resolve which he formed to rid himself of Dunkirk – to which I would never have agreed if it had not been for the King [of France], for I have such a high regard of him, that after the interests of my brother, I would not serve any ever but his – I beg you to do anything you can to help us end this matter, given that it is impossible for us to do any more for our part.

I also commend to your notice the matter of my regiment, and I beg you to write to me informally, since you must think of me as someone who has a great friendship for you.

le l'argent pour remedier aux affaires
presents, en attendent le termes que
le Roy de France promete, je vous
prie assurer que sans cette necessite
presante que le Roy mon frere deussi
natte par toutes le conditions que
le Roy de France eut voulu, sa plus
fort passion la miene et celle de
Mr le Chancellier estant de lier
une estroitte amitié et liaison
d'interests ince bien ce que je m'assure
vous jugerez bien par la resolution
que le Roy mon frere a prise de se
deffere de Dunkerke, a quoy je n'eusse
jamais consenti, si ce n'eust esté
pour le Roy pour qui j'ay une

estime si particulier jusques les
interest du Roy mon frere je n'en
prendre jamais sont siens, je
vous prie de contribuer attant que
vous pourres a la conclusion de cette
affaire estant impossible que nous
puissions faire d'avantage de notre
coste, je vous recomende aussi l'affaire
de mon Regiment, et vous prie de
ne me plus escrire avec ceremonie
puisque vous me aves regarder comme
un qui a beaucoup d'amitie pour
vous.

Restoration

LORD HIGH ADMIRAL

Convoyed home by ships of the still nominally Republican fleet, on 25 May 1660 Charles II landed with James at Dover. Four days later the new King was welcomed back into London by tumultuous crowds. The monarchy was restored on a wave of genuinely popular support, by a nation that had grown tired of almost constant warfare and upheavals in the State. However, the bare minimum of constraints was placed upon the King's powers and those of his ministers. More serious still, Anglicanism, reanimated with a militant and unforgiving spirit, would become the driving force behind the new 'Cavalier' Parliament of 1661 and would do much to define both the political and religious climate in England over the next twenty-five years by effectively proscribing both Protestant and Roman Catholic dissent.

Charles II enthroned as King, in 1661. Staring directly into the eyes of the viewer, with the orb and sceptre of state, and dressed in his coronation robes, Charles – as a new Solomon – consciously evokes the majesty and power of royal governance. It was an image appealing to continuity, rather than innovation, and harking back to the ideals of medieval kingship, that would serve Charles II well until the bitter gusts of the Exclusion swept over his throne. Artist: John Wright.

In the meantime, however, with all thought of foreign service now abandoned, James at last came into his inheritance and took up the reigns of power at the Navy Office in his capacity of Lord High Admiral of England. Samuel Pepys, as Clerk to the Navy Board, initially scoffed at the Duke's habitual lateness for meetings but soon came to report enthusiastically upon his ability to chair the discussions and to take advice from the more experienced sailors present. James prided himself on being an authority on shipbuilding. He kept a highly detailed pocket book in which he recorded information on the naval establishment, and he assembled a large library of charts and nautical books for his own use and for the instruction of his growing team of civil servants. As both the

Crown and his own household sank further into debt, James came to believe that he could combine his own private, mercantile interests with a scheme for the enrichment of the nation. This involved the seizure of existing colonies and the domination of foreign trade routes by the aggressive projection of English naval power. Having invested heavily in plans to open up the west coast of Africa in search of gold and slaves and sponsored attempts to reinvigorate the English fisheries, James soon came to perceive that the commercial and maritime strength of the Dutch Republic presented a major stumbling block to his ambitions.

James as Lord High Admiral, in 1672, by Henri Gascars. The painting was commissioned to celebrate his victory at the Battle of Sole Bay, and shows James in the guise of Mars, the God of War, with the English fleet waiting expectantly upon his command. Confident, powerful, and ambitious for further glory, the prince was unaware that within a matter of months he would be removed from the Admiralty and stripped of all his public offices.

Consequently, he put himself at the head of a war party in the Privy Council. He pressed his brother to launch a pre-emptive strike against the Dutch in the belief that a spectacular victory could be quickly and cheaply obtained. James's own father-in-law, Sir Edward Hyde – who had recently been ennobled as the Earl of Clarendon – despaired of his impetuousness and commented in his memoirs that 'his nature inclined to the most difficult and dangerous enterprises, [and] was already weary of having so little to do, and too impatiently longed for any war, in which he could not but have the chief command'.

However, despite all of Clarendon's warnings, punitive raids were despatched against the Dutch holdings in Africa and America. These resulted in the conquest of New Amsterdam and its renaming as New York in James's honour. The Duke became the colony's proprietor, answerable only to the King for his actions. He had the power to appoint his own officials to the territory, to raise taxes and to sit in judgment on court cases that affected the settlers. In this manner, he ruled New York as though it were his own private fiefdom, without recourse to representative assemblies, until he was overthrown in 1688.

Dutch Attack on the Medway: The Royal Charles Carried into Dutch Waters 12 June, 1667, by Ludolf Bakhuizen (1667). With the Dutch colours run up at its stern, the Royal Charles is taken as a Dutch prize and carried away, in the worst and most needless defeat ever suffered by the Royal Navy. Writing as the dockyards and stores still smouldered, John Evelyn thought it: 'A dreadful spectacle as ever Englishmen saw and a dishonour never to be wiped off!'

Hoping to lure the Dutch navy away from protecting its home ports and thereby to force a decisive confrontation, James led out the English battle fleet in an impressive display of strength and dropped anchor off the coast of Suffolk. With his foes readily accepting the bait, battle was joined at Lowestoft on 3 June 1665. James soon found himself in the thick of the action. His flagship directly engaged and destroyed that of his Dutch counterpart, Admiral van Opdam. He failed to follow up his advantage, however, and the rest of the enemy fleet was allowed to escape under the cover of darkness. Thus, the battle proved inconclusive. The heavy casualties suffered, especially among the officers and nobility, made Charles II fear for his brother's safety. Consequently, he refused to allow him to continue hazarding his life in an active command. He sent him instead to the north of England to keep a watch upon would-be Republican plotters there, and to keep him safe from both Dutch bullets and the plague which was ravaging his capital and the Home Counties.

The war and, indeed, the affairs of the nation went from bad to worse. The Dutch continued to more than hold their own at sea, draining the State coffers of funds and bringing Charles II's government close to bankruptcy. Then on 2 September 1666 the embers from an unattended oven set fire to a shop in Pudding Lane. The conflagration soon spread to engulf almost the entire City of London. Though James attempted to control the inferno by pulling down houses to create fire-breaks in its path, such measures proved largely ineffectual. Four nights later the begrimed and blackened Duke looked out upon the remains of what had been Europe's largest metropolis, now reduced to a series of stark ruins and scorched timbers.

Just as serious was the raid by the Dutch fleet, in June of the following year, upon the royal dockyards on the Thames and the

A contemporary Dutch map, showing the extent of the raid up the Rivers Thames and Medway, 7–14 June 1667. Sheerness was stormed and Chatham burned. The officials at the Royal Dockyards fled at the first sign of trouble, and English soldiers and sailors – who had gone unpaid and starved for many months – refused to fight, while Dutch raiding parties feasted on sheep taken on the Isle of Sheppey. (The map is drawn with south at the top).

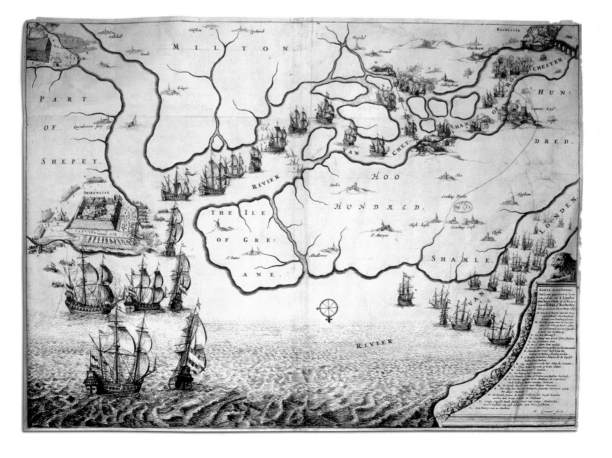

River Medway. Chatham was burned, along with three warships at their moorings, while the flagship of the English navy – *The Royal Charles* – was towed back to Holland as a triumphant prize. It was a dreadful humiliation, and one for which James was partly to blame. He had argued against standing down the fleet and returning the vessels to their docks, as a money-saving measure in expectation of a signing of the peace, but he had failed to ensure that the dockyards were adequately protected. He also did nothing, once the Dutch attack had actually begun, to rally his panic-stricken sailors or to salvage the situation.

A scapegoat was needed for the loss of the war. Lord Clarendon's aristocratic opponents seized their chance to discredit him and to blame him for the defeats and endemic government corruption, despite the fact that he had consistently spoken out for peace. Though the relationship between James and his thoughtful and scholarly father-in-law had not always been easy, he tried to protect him from charges of treachery and graft. Unfortunately, as the parliamentary debates about the Chancellor's future reached their height, James was struck down by smallpox. He voted against Lord Clarendon's impeachment – to his brother's great displeasure – but could do nothing to prevent his fall. With the Earl fled into exile, James was henceforth denied his temperate counsel and removed from his circle of High Anglican friends.

THE CONVERT

Illness had forced James to confront his own mortality, and his removal from active command now afforded him the time and leisure to investigate more fully those religious problems, and doctrinal differences, which had always troubled him. Unable to approach Clarendon, James turned instead to his wife, Anne, for help and advice.

The couple had met during their exile upon the Continent. James had had other mistresses, but Anne quickly established a dominant place in his

The House of York by Gennari after Lely. With no legitimate heir to succeed the King, James's own family took on an ever-greater prominence. Here he is shown with his first wife, Anne Hyde, and their two daughters, Mary and Anne. Cradling the globe, James reminds the onlooker of his colonial conquests and mercantile projects. His children guaranteed the future of the monarchy and his own fame looked set to spread across the entire world.

affections and prevailed upon him to offer her the promise of marriage. To the horror of her father, Lord Clarendon, Anne fell pregnant and, after the restoration of the monarchy, demanded that James made good upon his promise to her. Twisting this way and that, James did everything he could to get out of the match but, surprisingly, Charles II decided that his brother should be held to his word. The ceremony was conducted in the dead of night in front of only a handful of witnesses. While the marriage did little to halt James's habitual cycle of infidelities, the couple showed respect and affection towards one another, and their rapidly growing family served as a highly visible – and often noisy – contrast to the King's own, barren, marriage bed.

Spurred on by Anne, who had already converted to Roman Catholicism, James began to read up on church history. He was horrified by his discovery that the schism that had led to the creation of the Church of England seemed to have had its origins purely in the desire of Henry VIII to obtain a divorce from Catherine of Aragon. With Anglicanism thus discredited in his eyes, James turned instead to the Roman Catholic Church, which he believed might alone claim infallibility (see Document 4, *James's reasons for his conversion*). Having once made up his mind to change his faith, James never subsequently wavered in his decision. His conversion to Roman Catholicism served as the defining moment in both his personal life and public career. It rendered him suspect to a large proportion of his brother's subjects and raised questions about the nature of his conduct and the eventual succession to the throne that would destabilise English politics for the next two decades. Yet as James took his first Catholic communion, he appears to have been singularly unprepared for the storms that would overtake him when news of his conversion became public, and he was transformed from 'the darling of the Nation, for having so freely and so often ventured his life for the honour of the King and Country', to 'the common enemy' to be set upon from all sides.

THE LOSS OF OFFICE AND THE GAINING OF A NEW BRIDE

With an enormous government debt to service, Charles II turned not to his own troublesome Parliament for support, but to the financial and military might of Louis XIV. The subsequent alliance was concluded at Dover in 1670 in an atmosphere of the utmost secrecy. It pledged Charles II to convert to Roman Catholicism and to work to ensure that all of his subject peoples also returned

Holding the potential either to tear the Stuart monarchy apart, or to impose Roman Catholicism upon the English people with the force of French arms, the Secret Treaty of Dover represented an enormous political risk. Charles II had gained financial solvency and independence at the price of jeopardising both his crown and the well being of the English Catholic minority. He made sure that his leading Catholic courtiers; Lords Arlington, Arundell and Clifford, together with the Queen's secretary – Sir Richard Bellings – signed the paper, but pointedly refused to allow James to take a direct part in the venture.

aussy tost qu'il le pourra et qu'il en sera requis en foy de
quoy les dits sieurs commissaires et Ambassadeur ont
signé le present traité et a iceluy fait apposer le cachet
de leurs armes. a Douvres ce vingt et deuxiesme jour du
mois de may l'an de grace mil six cens soixante et dix.

Arlington

Colbert

T. Arundel
T. Clifford
R. Bellings

Charles R

Charles par la grace de dieu Roy de la Grande Bretagne
France et Irelande defenseur de la foye, a tous ceux qui
ces presentes lettres verront Salut. ayans leu et meurement
consideré les pouvoirs du sieur Colbert Ambassadeur de nostre
tres cher et tres amé Frere et Cousin le Roy treschrestien
dattés du 21 d'octobre 1669 par les quels nostre dit Frere luy
donne autorité de conferer avec les commissaires que nous
pourrions nommer, traitter, conclurre, et signer des articles
d'une plus estroicte amitie, liaison, et confederation entre
nous, et declare que nulle autre alliance ne luy peut estre
plus agreable ny plus auantageuse a ses sujets: nous qui
sommes dans les mesmes dispositions, et qui n'auons point
de desir plus ardent que de nous lier d'une amitie parfaite
et indissoluble avec nostre dit Frere, y estant conuiés et par
la proximité du sang. l'affection et estime que nous auons
pour

4 *James's reasons for his conversion*

James wrote down this explanation of his innermost thoughts in the late 1690s, for the benefit of his son's religious education.

Though he had once attended mass in Brussels, 'for the sake of the music', admired the loyalty of Catholics to his father's cause, and been greatly impressed by his conversation with a nun on the subject of salvation while on service in Flanders, it was not until he reached the threshold of middle age that James's thoughts began to turn towards religion. Profoundly unimaginative and possessed of an authoritarian tempera-ment, he desired social and religious order and sought rigid doctrinal certainties from an unchanging and infallible Church. With his faith in Anglicanism shattered by his wife's revelations, he moved to embrace Rome and became convinced of its correctness after a series of discussions with a Jesuit priest in 1669. However, it was probably not until the early 1670s that he was formally received into the Church and word of his conversion became public knowledge.

During his final exile, James outlined the reasons behind his conversion and emphasised what he felt to be the corro-sive effect of Protestantism upon the fabric of society. Rebellion and revolution seemed to him to stem directly from a crisis of spiritual authority. Only adherence to a single Church, which drew its authority directly from Christ through the apostolic succession, could ensure stability and the survival of a rigidly stratified society, in which monarchy could function and flourish.

With this in mind, in the late 1690s James recalled his reasons for converting for the benefit of his young son and his remaining followers at the chateau of Saint Germain-en-Laye.

JAMES WROTE:

you nor nobody ought to wonder that there are such alterations made in the Church of England as established by Law [rather than by God], every day, since those who come after the first reformers, have as much authority to reform again as those who began [the process], nay much more, for if some few members of the Church of England when united to the Catholic and Apostolic Church took upon them to fall off and separate themselves from the body of the Universal Church: how can those of the present Church of England, as they call themselves, find fault with such of their body, or others, who would reform upon them? Till they began the schism all was quiet as to religion in our unfortunate country, but since all the world sees what disorders it has caused and how our islands have been overrun with diversities of sects in the Church and with ruin and rebellion in the State, when people set ill out at first and mistake their way, it is no wonder if they …

He continued:

go still more and more astray.

you nor nobody aught to wonder that there are
such alterations ^made in the Ch: of Eng: as establisht
by Law, ever day, since those who come after
the first reformers, have as much authority
to reforme againe as those who began, nay
much more, for if some ^few members of the Ch: of
Eng: when united to the ^ Cath: and Apos: Ch:,
took upon them to fall off and seperat them
selues from the body of the oninersal Ch:,
how can those of the present Ch: of Eng:, as
they call themselues, find fault with
such of their body, or others, who would
reforme upon them, till they began the ^Schisme
all was quiet ^as to Religion in our unfortunat country,
but since all the world sees what disorders
it has caused and how our ^ Hands haue been
over run with diuersites of sects in the
Ch: and with ruine and Rebellion in the
state, when people sett ill out at first and
mistake there way, tis no wonder if they

to the faith, in return for generous annual subsidies from the French Crown. King Charles had little inclination to deliver upon his side of the bargain, but the immediate effect was to propel England, as France's sworn ally, into a fresh war of aggression against Holland.

James rejoined his battle fleet, which now included the ships of his French allies, at Sole Bay but was surprised, as the fog lifted over the North Sea, by the sudden approach of the Dutch squadrons. Despite an initial advantage in numbers, he only barely hung on until nightfall, engaging in a bloody artillery duel that badly mauled both fleets but yielded no real advantage to either side. Though he was anxious to renew the campaign at the start of the following year, the collapse of his political fortunes prevented him from doing so.

It was now common knowledge that James had stopped taking Anglican communion and become a Roman Catholic. Parliament, critical of the King's financial mismanagement, failure to win the war and toleration of religious dissent, moved to strip him of his Catholic advisors. The Test Act, passed in March 1673, compelled every holder of public office to swear allegiance to the Anglican Church and to explicitly deny the Catholic belief in transubstantiation. This James, in all conscience, could not do. So, with tears in his eyes, he surrendered all of his commands to his brother three months later and very dramatically retreated back into private life, throwing himself into the pursuit of sports and hunting (see Document 5, *The royal huntsman*).

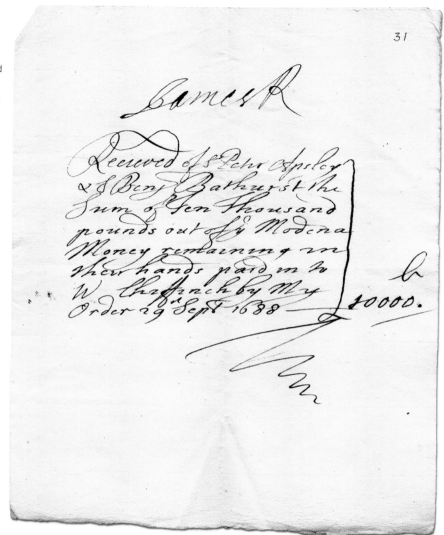

The non-payment of Mary of Modena's dowry haunted James for many years. Both her brother and uncle were seemingly unwilling, or unable, to pay it in full, with sums trickling in, piecemeal, over the next fifteen years. Here, just weeks before the landing of William of Orange, James is still kept busy apportioning the funds. Ironically, it would be William – as King – who set forth the most comprehensive scheme for her maintenance.

Though her earliest ambition was to become a nun, and her faith bordered upon bigotry, Mary of Modena was vivacious and charming in equal measure, as is firmly attested to by this miniature of her, painted in 1677, by Peter Cross. She would remain a pillar of strength and reassurance to her husband, despite all of their subsequent misfortunes.

Newly widowed, he sent his emissaries out across Europe to find him a royal bride. To the fury of his parliamentary critics, James chose the beautiful sister of the Duke of Modena, who was not only a devout Roman Catholic but also from a family that had traditionally allied itself with the power of France. The 15-year-old Mary of Modena arrived at Dover tearful and bewildered at the prospect of marriage to an already middle-aged man, but in fact the match proved agreeable and a deep love grew up between the pair that only improved with time.

5 The royal huntsman

A letter from James to Prince William of Orange, 7 October 1678.

The pursuit of field sports offered James the opportunity to escape from his troubles and his increasingly onerous workload. It afforded him the exercise and excitement that he had missed ever since his military career had been brought to an unexpected close by the passage of the First Test Act. He spent much of his time in the saddle, as both Duke and King, riding to the hounds two or even three days a week. He even received the news of his mother's death while out hunting in the New Forest with Charles II.

Samuel Pepys thought him 'a very desperate huntsman' and noted that no obstacle, whatever its size, was permitted to impede his progress across country. However, such an attitude was not without its dangers. At the start of the season in 1676, James, to his intense annoyance, was confined to bed by his doctors for a period of recuperation after a fall from his horse had broken his collarbone.

Moreover, the Restoration court was a very restricted place, revolving about the cultural and social life of the capital and only moving – save for natural disasters, such as plague and fire – to accommodate the royal brothers' love for sports and the racing season at Newmarket. Even when James's choice of religion began to elicit open criticism and rumours of Roman Catholic plots began to destroy the cohesion of the ruling elite in Parliament, he could still find time to pursue his quarry across the fields of Cambridgeshire and Suffolk. He regaled his nephew – and new son-in-law – William of Orange with tales of his exploits, as in this letter written from Newmarket.

THE LETTER READS:

I received yours of the 6th [New Style] of this month since I came hither, where we have had very bad weather, which has made this place be duller than it used to be, and has hindered his Majesty from hawking some days, but not me from fox hunting. There has yet been few races, but tomorrow they begin again and there will be some for every day so long as we stay here. His Majesty has not yet named the day he intends to go back to …

The letter continues over the page:

London, but I believe it will be about the middle of next week. When Parliament meet, we shall see what they will do and then must take our measures accordingly.

Newmarkett Octo: 7: 128 1678

I receued yours of the 6: of this
month since I came hether, where
we haue had very bad weather
which has made this place be
duller then it uses to be, and
has hindred his Ma: from hawking
some dayes but not me from fox
hunting, there has yett been few
races, but tomorrow they begin
againe and there will be some for
every day so long as we stay
here, his Ma: has not yett named
the day he intends to go back to

66

POPISH PLOT AND EXCLUSION CRISIS

Deprived of office and fearing the increasingly authoritarian policies propounded by James and his friend the Earl of Danby, the King's key advisors, a growing band of Parliamentarians began to gather about the Earl of Shaftesbury. They argued that James represented a direct threat to the lives and liberty of his brother's subjects and should therefore be stripped of his right to inherit the throne, possibly in favour of the King's illegitimate son, the Duke of Monmouth. Today it may seem incomprehensible that a personal choice of religion might be enough to bar an individual from office or to shake the foundations of government. But in the late seventeenth century, when the powers of the King were still growing, much depended upon the personality of the sovereign, and what was religious was also, without a shadow of doubt, political. English Protestants, whether Anglicans, Presbyterians or Independents, had long memories and shared a common tradition of having once been a persecuted minority, reviled as heretics and hunted down and burned on the orders of a Roman Catholic sovereign. With James increasingly identified with the use of military power, many were prepared to believe that, if he came to the throne, he would force his subjects to convert to Catholicism.

Unfortunately, the crude association of Roman Catholicism with all that was criminal, disloyal or just plain disturbing permitted an unscrupulous appeal to society's basest and most irrational fears – the hatred of strangers and of distinct subcultures – and turned legitimate political grievances into a mindless, and raging, form of popular hysteria.

Thus, the fevered allegations of Titus Oates, concerning a 'Popish Plot' to bring down the State, fell upon remarkably fertile ground.

As ungainly and slow in body as he was corrupt and quick of mind, Titus Oates was jailed for lying on oath in 1673. He lost his living as a curate but escaped from prison and, in 1675, took ship for Tangier as a naval chaplain. Discharged for misconduct within months, he took service in the Duke of Norfolk's predominantly Catholic household, as pastor to his Protestant servants. There he gained valuable insights into the life of the English Catholic community, which added plausibility to his later allegations. Even at the beginning of the nineteenth century, as shown by this engraving, he was still being hailed in some quarters as a Protestant 'hero'.

TITUS OATES, D.D.

The first Discoverer of the Plot.

Pub.d Aug.t 25. 1813 by R.S.Kirby 11 London House Yard.

was upon a *Habeas Corpus* admitted to Bail, and afterwards obtain'd the King's Pardon.

Titus Oats, being Tryed and Convicted on Two several In- *Titus Oats*
dictments of Perjury, he was Sentenced to be Deprived of his *Convicted of*
Canonical Habit for ever, to stand in the Pillory at *Westminster-* *Perjury.*
Hall-Gate and at the *Royal-Exchange*, to be Whipt from *Ald-*
gate to *Newgate*, and from *Newgate* to *Tyburn* : To stand in the *His Sentence*
Pillory Five Days every Year during his Life, and that he Pay
a Fine of 1000 Marks, and suffer Imprisonment during his
Life.

On May 20. Thomas Dangerfield was Try'd and Convicted for

As Sandford's laconic *A Genealogical History of the Kings and Queens of England* (1707) notes, after his accession to the throne, James attempted a reckoning with those who dared to oppose him. Yet, here he was to be thwarted. Unlike Monmouth's humbler followers, Lords Delamere and Stamford had powerful friends and were acquitted of all charges, while the blows that were intended to kill Titus Oates merely scarred and striped his back. He emerged from prison after the Revolution and continued to fabricate new stories of plots, though to diminishing returns.

Through the summer and autumn of 1678 rumour fed upon rumour, culminating in an enormous public outcry over the suspicious death of a popular London magistrate (see Document 6, *The death of Magistrate Godfrey*). The Catholics were falsely blamed. But even though Charles II had already exposed the inconsistencies in Oates' statements, he refused to condemn him as an outright charlatan. Instead, he preferred that the mob should expend its fury upon a handful of elderly peers and the Jesuit priests seized in raids across the capital, rather than allowing too close an examination of his own, decidedly murky, affairs.

The scope of the allegations widened still further to include James's former secretary, Edward Coleman, a Roman Catholic convert. Coleman had rashly boasted in his correspondence with the French court that England might yet be recovered from 'heresy and schism'. To make matters worse, he was arrested while trying to burn the incriminating letters. It was only the intervention of Danby, who heavily censored their text before making them public, that saved James from being incriminated and dragged down along with his indiscreet servant. Having sworn on his honour before both the House of Lords and the Privy Council that he had had no knowledge of the correspondence carried on in his name, James abandoned the unfortunate secretary to his fate. Coleman went to a traitor's death at Tyburn, expecting till the last that a pardon might still come as a reward for having kept faith with his master.

As criticism of James mounted and charges of treason were prepared against Danby, the King dissolved Parliament in order to gain a brief respite and to ensure that his brother might be safely placed out of harm's way before a newly elected House of Commons had the chance to deliberate upon his future. James had initially refused to go quietly and urged the King to use the army to stage a *coup d'état* against the opposition, but he was eventually persuaded to take ship for the Low Countries. There he visited his daughter, Mary, who had been married to Prince William of Orange as a sop to Protestant opinion, and repeatedly grumbled about his brother's supposed weakness.

He could only look on as, at the general election of February 1679, the opposition won a clear majority in the Commons, greatly emboldening Shaftesbury and his Whig followers and sharpening both the scope and the sting of their subsequent legislative campaign. Henceforth, they committed themselves to nothing less than the exclusion of the Duke of York from ever succeeding to the throne – in a clear assault upon the hereditary principle – his permanent removal from all levers of power, and his treatment before the law as a common criminal, liable to the same fines and penalties for non-attendance at church as any private subject.

Charles II's sudden illness in August brought James back from exile, but the King's full recovery and the passions that the Duke's presence still stirred among the people ensured that he was not allowed to stay at his side for long. However, even though James was an enormous political liability while in England, the King realised that he might be a positive asset north of the border, where a long-running rebellion against the Crown still smouldered. Consequently, over the course of two protracted stays in Scotland, James acted as his brother's High Commissioner, stamping out dissent, centralising the administration and carefully leading the deliberations of a largely nominated Scots Parliament. Though he made a powerful enemy of the Earl of Argyll, James was able to chart a careful and largely successful course. He kept out of the sight and mind of his English critics, while guaranteeing Scottish loyalty

A letter from James to Prince William of Orange, 18 October 1678.

Concerned about the health of his eldest daughter, who had miscarried and was unhappy at The Hague, James had, in October 1678, sent his wife and daughter Anne to keep her company. However, if he thought that domestic concord had been re-established in his family, James had good reason to view the new session of Parliament, in the autumn of 1678, with

mounting trepidation. Since the summer, stories had been circulating that the King was to be assassinated while out walking in St James's Park and that an invasion force, financed by the Pope and Louis XIV, was to conquer the English State, aided by a powerful fifth column of Jesuits and Catholic grandees. Unfortunately, the disappearance of Magistrate Godfrey, shortly after he had taken sworn evidence of the plot from Titus Oates, appeared

to point to the truth of a conspiracy.

In discussing matters with his nephew, James correctly dismissed the plot as a work of fiction and accurately identified both its targets and its genesis in the popular hatred of Catholics. He provided William of Orange with a factual account of the discovery of Godfrey's corpse in this letter written from Whitehall.

THE LETTER READS:

We came hither on Wednesday from Newmarket, and the same night presently after the 11th the Duchess arrived, so satisfied with her journey and with you as I never saw anybody, and I must give you a thousand thanks from her and from myself for her kind usage by you. I should say more on this subject, but I am very ill at compliments and you care not for them.

The pretended plot is still under examination and the judges are to give their opinion, whether one witness in point of treason be sufficient to proceed criminally against anybody, and I verily believe that, when this affair is thoroughly examined, it will be found nothing but malice against the poor Catholics in general and myself in particular.

Another thing has happened, which is that a J.P., Sir Edmondbury Godfrey, was missing some days, suspected by several circumstances, very probable ones, to design the making himself away. Yesterday his body was found in a by-place, in the fields two or three miles off, with his own sword through him. This makes a great noise, and is laid against the Catholics also, but without any reason for it, for he was known to be far from being an enemy to them.

All these things happening together will cause, I am afraid, a great flame in the Parliament, when they meet on Monday, for those disaffected to the government will inflame all things as much as they can.

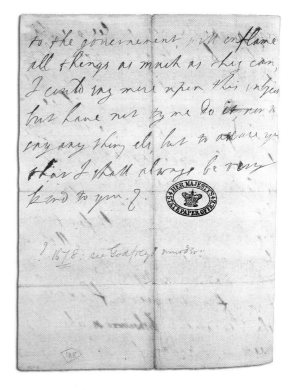

and remaining poised to lead an army south if the position of the monarchy was to deteriorate further. Safe from impeachment, he could now afford to wait for a more favourable time to fully reassert his rights.

COUNTER-REVOLUTION

During James's absence, Charles II had been far from idle. He mounted a skilful defence of his prerogatives and rallied his natural Tory supporters about the Crown. It was one thing to criticise the heir to the throne but, as Shaftesbury's supporters found to their cost, quite another to stand against the King, or to argue against the hereditary principle upon which all property rights were based. Even though two bills for James's exclusion were voted through the House of Commons, Charles still retained the right to call and to dissolve his Parliaments at will. He used these powers, in combination with his in-built majority in the House of Lords, to prevent the legislation from passing into law.

While Shaftesbury and his supporters had no trouble in agreeing that James lay at the root of the nation's troubles and should be prevented from becoming King at all costs, they lacked a common approach to tactics and could not decide upon who – or, indeed, what – should replace him after his place in the succession was denied. By ordering a series of well-timed prorogations of Parliament, Charles II was able to disrupt the momentum of the opposition's campaign before delivering his masterstroke. By transferring Parliament to Oxford in March 1681, he removed radical MPs from their power base in London and confined them to an unfamiliar, and largely hostile, setting. Having ringed the city with troops, the

King's sudden and unexpected dismissal of his final Parliament was coupled with the removal of *Habeus Corpus* and a prolonged assault upon the municipal authorities. As charter after charter was stripped away from the militant cities and Crown representatives were directly appointed, the opposition MPs meekly returned home and the Common Council of London was disbanded.

The Great Seal of Charles II, 1672. The obverse, with the king enthroned, ready to dispense justice and to act as a beacon of virtue, faithfully echoes the messages of his coronation portrait. However, the reverse, showing Charles riding to war vividly demonstrates the king's other functions, as the crusher of faction and dissent, and as the leader of an increasingly formidable and professional army. By the 1680s, it was in these latter roles that Charles came increasingly to be seen, as he countenanced the use of force at Oxford and sat for portraits in armour for the first time since the Restoration.

In effect, Charles II had called the Whigs' bluff and they, fearing a renewal of civil war, had fatally blinked. Though a London jury acquitted Shaftesbury of treason, his support haemorrhaged away and he was forced to seek refuge in Holland, an ailing and increasingly forlorn figure (see Document 7, *The Tory reaction*). With the opposition shattered and Parliament having broken up, a handful of English Republicans discussed assassinating Charles and James as the prelude to a general rising. However, it is doubtful if their plans amounted to anything more than vague talk and wild hopes. They were quickly captured and sentenced to death (see Document 8, *The opposition crushed*).

James had already returned to London in triumph, picking up the threads of the naval administration that he had been forced to lay down almost a decade before. With government finances restored, no pressing need to recall Parliament and the principle of divine-right monarchy firmly reasserted, Charles II's power and prestige appeared unchallengeable. However, fate was now to intervene to lay him in his grave and to place his shocked and saddened brother unexpectedly upon the throne (see Document 9, *The death of King Charles II*).

7 *The Tory reaction*

A letter from James to Prince William of Orange, 18 December 1682.

The Whig Party, which had coalesced about the Earl of Shaftesbury and the Duke of Monmouth and looked poised to complete a constitutional revolution, barring James from the succession to the throne, collapsed in ruins after the dissolution of the Oxford Parliament. As local government was overhauled and the remaining Whigs were purged from the corporations, the power of the monarchy dramatically reasserted itself. The improvement in government finances, resulting from an increase in foreign trade, enabled Charles II to dispense with the services of Parliament for the remainder of his reign and to lay the foundations, in terms of a growing military establishment and a tightly controlled judiciary, for the creation of a viable absolutist system.

As plans for military risings in Cheshire and the west and the pre-emptive seizure of the Tower fizzled out, the Tories completed their triumph by having their candidates elected as Sheriffs of London in 1682. With Monmouth under arrest and his foes now able to hand-pick the juries called to deliver verdicts upon his activists, Shaftesbury realised that he would not be acquitted if he stood trial for treason a second time. This knowledge prompted his flight to Holland in November 1682 and his last attempts to rally the now fragmented, and increasingly Republican, opposition from there.

James's disappointment that his chief foe had escaped from his clutches, and his sense of frustration that the spirit of democracy and toleration espoused by the Dutch Republic would make it difficult for his nephew to apprehend and return the fugitive nobleman for trial, were keenly felt and passionately expressed. However, these sentiments were counterbalanced by the knowledge that the Exclusionist challenge had failed and that, save for a small nucleus of Republicans, the remaining Whigs had been silenced and forced tacitly to accept his eventual succession to the throne.

The struggle for the post of Lord Chancellor, left vacant by the death of the Earl of Nottingham, though hotly contested, did not lead to a re-ignition of factional politics. In 1683 the post was filled, as James had predicted, by the universally respected figure of Sir Francis North.

This letter was written from Windsor.

THE LETTER READS:

I find by yours of the 22nd [New Style], which I had yesterday at London, that Lord Shaftesbury was at Amsterdam and do easily believe that you will have nothing to do with such a kind of man as he, that is so very great an enemy to all our family in general, as well as a particular one to me. I am told that many of the Fanatic party flock to him, and no doubt to his power, he will do his part to do what harm he can to us. We came from London this morning, where I do not know whether the Lord Chancellor were alive or dead, he being speechless last night. 'Tis believed that Lord Chief Justice North will succeed him, who is both able and bold, as well as very loyal. We have had hitherto a very gentle winter and 'tis …

The letter concludes:

like to continue so.

Windsor Dec: 18: 1682   144

I find by yours of the 22: which I had
yesterday at Long that L. Shaftsbury
was at Amsterdam, and do verily beleeve
that you will have nothing to do with
such a kind of man as he, that is so very
great an enemy to all our family in
generall as well as a particular one to me,
I am told that many of the Phanatike party
flock to him, and no doubt, to his power,
he will do his part to ~~~~~ do what harme
he can, to us, wee came from London this
morning, where I do not know whether
the L. Chancelor, wee alive or dead, he
being speechlesse last night, tis beleeved that
L. Ch: Jus: North will succeede him, who is both
able and bold, as well as very Loyal, we have
had hitherto a very gentil winter, and tis

104

A letter from James to Prince William of Orange, 9 November 1683.

Shaftesbury's departure had created a vacuum at the centre of the Whig opposition, which was only partially filled by the reappearance in London of Algernon Sidney, a Republican and far-sighted political theorist. Sidney had consistently advocated the overthrow of the monarchy and hoped that coordinated risings in England could be assisted by the arrival of Scottish rebels, under the command of the Earl of Argyll, but his plans had not got very far. Few arms had been stockpiled and he was arrested on 26 June 1683, while still working away at his book on the nature of government. It was alleged that he and his aristocratic co-conspirators, who joined him in the Tower, had planned to attack Charles and James as they rode back from Newmarket to London. A farm cart was to have blocked the narrow way outside the gates of Rye House in Hertfordshire. While the royal guards stopped to move it, the conspirators were to have peppered the convoy with shot from the cover of the surrounding hedgerows, bringing down both brothers. However, there is no evidence to suggest that the Rye House Plot amounted to anything more than careless and wishful talk, magnified greatly by government informants hankering after an amnesty or financial reward. This made both the indictment of Sidney and his subsequent trial extremely difficult for the authorities, as there was little direct evidence to link him with the assassination plot. Indeed, only one witness, rather than the two required by law, could be brought against him. Nevertheless, the government promoted George Jeffreys to the rank of Lord Chief Justice in September 1683, in the sole knowledge that he would stop at nothing to secure a conviction. Sidney was thus arraigned on 7 November, and the date of his trial was set for a fortnight later.

James knew full well that the outcome was a forgone conclusion and saw in Sidney's death the final crushing of the Whig movement and the end of a specifically Republican threat. He cared not, or simply did not observe, that, as he returned to the hunting field, his brother, a far more astute politician, was attempting to absolve himself of all responsibility for Sidney's trial and was letting it be known that it was James alone who had desired the colonel's blood.

What did concern James was the prospect of a fresh confrontation in Europe that would pitch France, once more, against the Dutch Republic and eventually compel England to take sides in a war that neither he nor his brother desired. To this end, and in the knowledge that the Turkish armies, though recently defeated outside Vienna, still threatened in the East, on 9 November 1683 he wrote to William of Orange from London with the latest news and the suggestion that the English might act as intermediaries and so prevent a further escalation of the war in the Low Countries.

THE LETTER READS:

Last night I received yours by Mr. Borstel of the 9th [New Style], and had before heard of the good news of the taking of Grave [a fortress on the River Meuse], and am as sorry as anybody can be that the war is begun in Flanders, and wish that while the winter lasts, some means of accommodation may be found, that all Christendom may be in peace. As for this country, all things go on very well, and Algernon Sidney has been tried by the grand jury, the bill found against him, and Wednesday come fortnight appointed for his trial. I was this day a fox-hunting, and since that at the Council, so that now I have not …

The letter continues:

time to say more, it being late, only to assure you that you shall still find me as kind to you as ever.

London Nou: 9: 1683.

Last night I receued yours by M: Borskel
of the 9:, and had before heard of the
good newse of the taking of Grave,
and am as sorry as any body can be
that the war is begun in flanders,
and wish that while the winter
lasts, some means of accomodation
may be found, that all Christendome
may be in peace, as for this country
all things go on very well, and Algernon
Sidney has been tryd by the grand
Jury, the bill found against him,
and wenesday come sennight apointed
for his tryal, I was this day a fox
hunting, and sence that at the
councell, so that now I haue not

The death of King Charles II

A brief letter from James to Prince William of Orange, 6 February 1685.

James worked best, and revealed his character in its finest light, when acting as a subordinate to another whom he respected, loved and admired. Thus, he had thrived under Marshal Turenne's tutelage and acted as his brother's trusted right-hand man for the quarter of a century that followed on from the Restoration of 1660. It was this overriding sense of loyalty to the Crown, and to the concept of an untainted and incontrovertible hereditary principle, that enabled James to pursue such an active political career across almost every sphere of government. It also permitted Charles II to entrust to him so many vitally important offices of State without fear of treachery or dissembling. Consequently, though during the Exclusion crisis he fought tooth and nail to preserve his own right to the succession, James never dreamed of contravening the equally legitimate rights of his brother to rule, or of openly opposing his wishes for any length of time. Content in his subordinate position, and in the reassuring knowledge that he – or more probably – one of his children would be called to the throne only in the far distant future, it came as a profound shock to James to find his brother suddenly gone, and the responsibilities of government thrust unexpectedly upon him.

The reasons behind such an assumption are not difficult to discern. Despite fears for his health in 1679 and 1680, King Charles had always appeared to be a strong and extremely active individual. He was expected – not least by his brother James – to live on into ripe old age. However, he was felled by a stroke on the morning of Monday 2 February 1685, and barbarously treated by his surgeons. While he was being bled and scalded, James rushed to his side in a state of panic, hardly stopping to throw off his dressing gown, pull on his boots and straighten his wig. On the fourth day of the King's illness, the French Ambassador noted that James was still behaving as though he were lost in a dream, and it was only when it was suggested that he summon a Catholic priest to administer the last rites that he finally pulled himself together. At the end, Charles II recalled his promise to Louis XIV and was received into the Church of Rome by the same priest who had sheltered him from Cromwell's troopers more than thirty years before. On the night that his brother died, James called for pen and ink and, abandoning all formality, scrawled a brief note to Prince William from Whitehall, informing him of his devastating loss.

THE LETTER READS:

I have only time to tell you, that it has pleased God Almighty to take out of this world the King, my brother. You will from others have an account of what distemper he died of, and, that all the usual ceremonies were performed this day in proclaiming me King, in the City and other parts. I must end, which I do with assuring you, you shall find me as kind to you as [you] can expect.

Whitehall Feb: 6: 1685 119

228

I have only tyme to tell you, that
it has pleased God Almighty, to
take out of this world, the King
my Brother, you will from others
have an account of what distemper
he dieed of, and that all the usuall
ceremonyes were performed this
day in proclaiming me King in this
Citty and other parts, I must end
which I do with assuring you, you
shall find me as kind to you as
con expect.

49

Jacobus Rex

THE NEW KING

James was crowned king, in Westminster Abbey, on St George's Day 1685, depicted in this 1697 colour engraving by William Sherwin. Temporary wooden galleries were built in the nave, in order to accommodate the enormous number of noble spectators who jostled for a glimpse of their new sovereign, and an enormous fireworks display lit up the Thames in celebration that night.

Francis Sandford, one of James's heralds, illustrated every aspect of the coronation ceremony. In this 1687 illustration, amid clouds of wafted incense, the musicians and choristers of the Chapel Royal join the procession to the Abbey.

Contrary to the fears of the Privy Council, James's succession in April 1685 was welcomed across the country with genuine celebration, unclouded by popular disturbances or by anything more serious than murmured dissent. The new King worked hard to reassure the Anglican elites that he would not tamper with the existing relationship between Church and State. He also promised that he would not seek to extend religious toleration to the non-conformist Protestant sects. Save for promoting his brother-in-law, Lord Rochester – a strong defender of both the Church of England and the Crown – to be his Lord Treasurer, he introduced few changes in his brother's ministerial team and showed little inclination to reopen the old wounds created by the Exclusion crisis.

Many of the Crown's most valuable sinecures had been granted only for the lifetime of Charles II and lapsed upon his death, but a financial and political crisis was averted by the calling of a fresh Parliament and by the energies of the King's election agents, who ensured that a large majority of loyal candidates were returned. Overwhelmingly dominated by the Tories and espousing the

frequently conjoined interests of the Anglican Church and landowners, the Commons gladly voted James II the large subsidies that he required for the smooth running of his government. These funds established the King's independence and placed him in the unique position, for a Stuart sovereign, of being debt free and in possession of an increasingly rich treasury. It was against this background of financial stability and general goodwill that James was able to meet the first challenge to his authority as King.

THE ROAD TO SEDGEMORE AND THE BLOODY ASSIZES

Forced into exile by the failure of the Exclusion campaign, the Duke of Monmouth had been in no position to press his claim to the throne immediately after the death of his father. However, as summer came on, he was able to raise sufficient money to buy weapons and armour and to equip two small vessels to transport him back to England. Believing that his landing would be accompanied by a series of risings in London, Scotland, Cheshire and the West Country, he set sail from Amsterdam at the end of May and came ashore at Lyme Regis (see Document 10, *Monmouth lands and raises a rebellion*).

Monmouth's uncompromisingly Protestant message and appeals for social justice struck an immediate chord with the artisans and labourers of the West Country, who rushed to join his newly sewn

This portrait, painted shortly after his victory against the Scottish rebels, in 1678, shows the Duke of Monmouth as an extremely good-looking and self-assured young man. However, he lacked any capacity for reflection and continually over-estimated both his own abilities and support among the political nation. Painted by Sir Godfrey Kneller.

colours. However, they did little to attract gentry support, and both Cheshire and the City of London failed to stir. The Earl of Argyll had already managed to land in Scotland, but his rebellion had quickly foundered amid general apathy and the torrential downpours that had accompanied his meandering progress through the Highlands. Cornered on the banks of the Clyde, he was separated from his dwindling band of adherents and captured, while Monmouth was forced to face the royal army alone.

The capture of the Earl of Argyll, by government forces, is shown in a contemporary Dutch print. He knew that he could expect no mercy from a vengeful king, and James II was to press remorselessly for his death.

Initially, Monmouth's rebels had enjoyed some success, attracting plentiful recruits and advancing swiftly through Devon and into Somerset without encountering any significant resistance from the local militias. However, Bristol refused to open its gates to welcome them. Monmouth, having lost his nerve, refused to sanction an attack upon the city and ordered a retreat. The initiative now passed to the royal army, which doggedly pursued the rebels back through Somerset before defeating them in the fields outside Bridgwater (see Document 11, *The Battle of Sedgemore*).

A letter from James to Prince William of Orange, 15 June 1685.

Both James and William of Orange had been wrong-footed by Monmouth's ability to raise and equip an expeditionary force from Amsterdam, and to successfully secure a passage across the Channel. The abject failure of the local militias to muster quickly and to intercept the rebels before they could march inland was a further cause of concern to the new King, and probably served to convince him of the need to recruit a large professional army in order to ensure his future security. The confused skirmish at Bridport on 12 June, which checked but did not break the rebel advance and left both sides claiming a victory, probably only served to confirm James's fears. In particular, Monmouth's declaration, in which he assumed the mantle of kingship and branded his uncle a traitor to the nation, enraged James and ensured that there could be no way back for either man. One of them would have to go down.

Pitched into an unexpected crisis, James reacted quickly. Parliament was fortunately still in session and voted large subsidies for the defeat of the rebellion, while setting a price of £5,000 upon Monmouth's head. Furthermore, battle-hardened troops, newly withdrawn from Tangier, were on hand and swiftly despatched to the west to join the command of the ablest of James's protégés, John Churchill. Time was on the King's side as he massed his forces, waiting on events in London and sifting the detailed intelligence reports that reached him with every post for news of his enemy's movements. This letter was written from Whitehall.

THE LETTER READS:

Though the Duke of Monmouth landed at Lyme in Dorsetshire on Thursday evening [11 June], I got no notice of it till Saturday morning. He found nobody in the town, I mean of the militia, and so possessed himself of it. Besides the ship he was in, himself, there came with him two other ships of about one hundred tons each, and by what I have been informed of, I do not hear he brought on shore with him above two hundred men, since which several of the common sort of people have flocked in to him, who he has armed, having brought with him great store, and by a spy I had lately [sent] amongst them, they give out they are three thousand, but he tells me they are not half so strong, and that then there …

The letter continues:

was never a gentleman came in to him, but one Trenchard that I had sent to seize some days before Monmouth's landing, and had got away, and was one of the late conspiracy with him, and had got out upon the Habeus Corpus Act. The militia of the neighbouring counties are by this got together, and [are] marching to him, and I have sent down nine companies of foot, four troops of horse, [and] two of dragoons, which are all to be at Salisbury by tomorrow night, with seven small field-pieces, to march forward if occasion be. There has been some little fighting already between the rebels and some of the Dorsetshire militia, at a place called Bridport, some three miles from Lyme, into which quarter, some two hundred foot, and one hundred horse of the rebels fell, and at first killed one Mr. Strangavais, and another gentleman, and took three or four more, but more help coming to the militia, they beat back the rebels, killed some, and took five, with several arms they flung away in their hasty retreat. This happened on Saturday, and every moment I hope to send you a good account of this affair. He [i.e. Monmouth] now takes upon him to be King, as you will see by the declaration he has put out, which by order of the Lords was burnt by the hands of the hangman. Sure there was never a more lying, malicious, paper than that. I was this day at the Parliament in my robes, and another for [the] attainting of the Duke of Monmouth, and I hope in a few days he will not be in a very good condition.

Whitehall June 15: 1685.   258

tho the D: of Monmouth landed at Lyme
in Dorcetshire, on thursday euening,
I gott not notice of it, till Saturday
morning, he found no body in the towne,
I meane of the militia, and so possest him
selfe of it, besids the ship he was in him
selfe, there came with him, two other
Ships, of about one hundred tuns each,
and by what I haue been yett informed
of, I do not heare, he brough on shoare w:th
him, aboue two hundred men, since
since seuerall of the common sort of
people, haue flocked into him, who he
has ermed, hauing brought with him
great store, and by a spy I had lately
amongst them, they giue out they are
three thousand, but he tells me they re
not halt so strong, and that then there

The Battle of Sedgemore

A letter from James to Prince William of Orange, 7 July 1685.

Audacity and speed were Monmouth's only remaining advantages, as his little army was pressed back into its original stronghold in Somerset. Accordingly, he conceived of a night attack upon the royal army, as it slept in the fields outside Bridgwater. Using a local guide, his regiments marched through the early hours of 5 July 1685, in silence and perfect order, until they came to the Langmoor Rhine, the first of two drainage ditches that separated them from the tented lines of the King's men. To Churchill's disappointment, the King had belatedly appointed Lord Feversham to lead the army. But as Monmouth's vanguard blundered into the royal scouts and the silence of the moor was punctured by warning shots, it was Churchill who was on hand to take charge of the situation. While Feversham slept on in a cottage to the rear, Churchill hastily formed his regiments into a firing line, ready to receive the rebel onslaught. Though Monmouth's troops had managed to cross the first ditch, amid the confusion they had lost their guide. They sought in vain for a way across the second dyke, known as the Bussex Rhine. A fierce fire-fight developed, which lasted until dawn, when the royal artillery finally thundered into action and Churchill sent his cavalry across the ditch to envelope the rebels and complete their rout.

Greatly relieved, King James sent word of the victory from Whitehall to William of Orange, providing him with a comprehensive and extremely accurate account of the battle, which reveals his skills as a military commentator to the full.

THE LETTER BEGINS:

I am sure it will please you very well to hear that it has pleased God to give my troops good success against the rebels here in England, as well as in Scotland. The Duke of Monmouth was got with all his troops to Bridgwater, and had summoned all the country to come in to him to fortify it; upon which Lord Feversham marched on Sunday last from Sommerton to a village called Weston [Zoyland], which is within some two or three miles of Bridgwater, near which he camped, with what he had of my old troops, which consisted of about two thousand foot, in six battalions, and some seven hundred horse and dragoons …

It then continues:

and eighteen small field pieces. The Earl of Pembroke with some horse and foot, of the militia were quartered in a village behind him, having not tents to camp with. On Sunday night the Duke of Monmouth came out of Bridgwater over the bridge, with all his troops, himself at the head of the foot, and Lord Grey commanded his horse, and came on with that great order and silence, that our parties which were out to see if he marched, did not hear him, and drew in battle upon the plain, and advanced straight on to our camp, hoping to surprise them, and about two in the morning engaged our foot with great vigour, and were as well received. They had but three pieces of cannon with them, which they brought up, within pistol shot of our foot. Our horse, in the meantime, drew up on the right hand of our foot, the left being so covered that they could not be taken by the flank, and charged the rebels' horse, which consisted of fifteen troops, and beat them at the first charge, but did not pursue them far, but fell back into the rear of the rebels foot, which made great resistance, but at last were all cut to pieces, their cannon, and two and twenty colours taken. How many were slain of them was not then known, nor how many prisoners …

The letter concludes:

just now I have heard from Lord Feversham, of last night of ten o'clock, in which he gives me an account that he was master of Bridgwater, that what horse of the rebels which escaped, had taken their way towards Bristol, that he had sent two parties of horse; the one to Cansham and the other to Bradford, to see to intercept them; that as to the Duke of Monmouth, he believed he got off only with forty horse. I have reason to believe now that the counties will rise upon them, so that he will have difficulty enough to get away. Lord Feversham has left some men in Bridgwater, and is marched to Wells, where he is this night. It is so late that I can say no more.

With the rebellion broken and Monmouth captured, alone and starving in a ditch, now should have been the time for clemency. James II, however, was not in a forgiving mood. Even though Monmouth had lost any support that he might once have enjoyed, in begging piteously for his life before the King and even promising to renounce his Protestantism for Rome, James showed no mercy and demanded that the death penalty be carried out. Worse still, he authorised his faithful servant, Judge Jeffreys, to carry out a series of brutal reprisals against the captive insurgents, designed to extirpate their cause and to teach the lower orders in general a graphic lesson about the price of treason. In addition to those who died in the fighting or of fever in overcrowded jails, 100 rebels were hung in the immediate aftermath of Sedgemore. A further 300 were hung, drawn and quartered on Jeffreys' orders, and 1,000 were sentenced to transportation to the West Indies. No individual appeal for clemency was permitted to the King, while his courtiers were able to make their fortunes by selling the prisoners to plantation owners.

James should have been reassured by the impressive loyalty shown to him by the propertied classes, and by the clinical efficiency of his regular forces. Instead, he recalled only the failures of his militia and sanctioned a massive increase in the professional army from roughly 7,000 men in 1685 to some 40,000 just three years later.

George Jeffreys at the height of his powers as Lord Chancellor. Abandoned by his master, in December 1688, he met his nemesis in the form of the London mob, who had neither forgotten nor forgiven his past cruelties. He was recognised by the crowd in Wapping, and only his swift committal to the Tower prevented his summary lynching.

The Right Hon.ble George Earle of Flint Viscount Weikham Baron of Weim I.st High Chancelour of England one of his Ma.ties most hon.ble Privy Councell.
G. Kneller pinx.   E. Cooper ex.

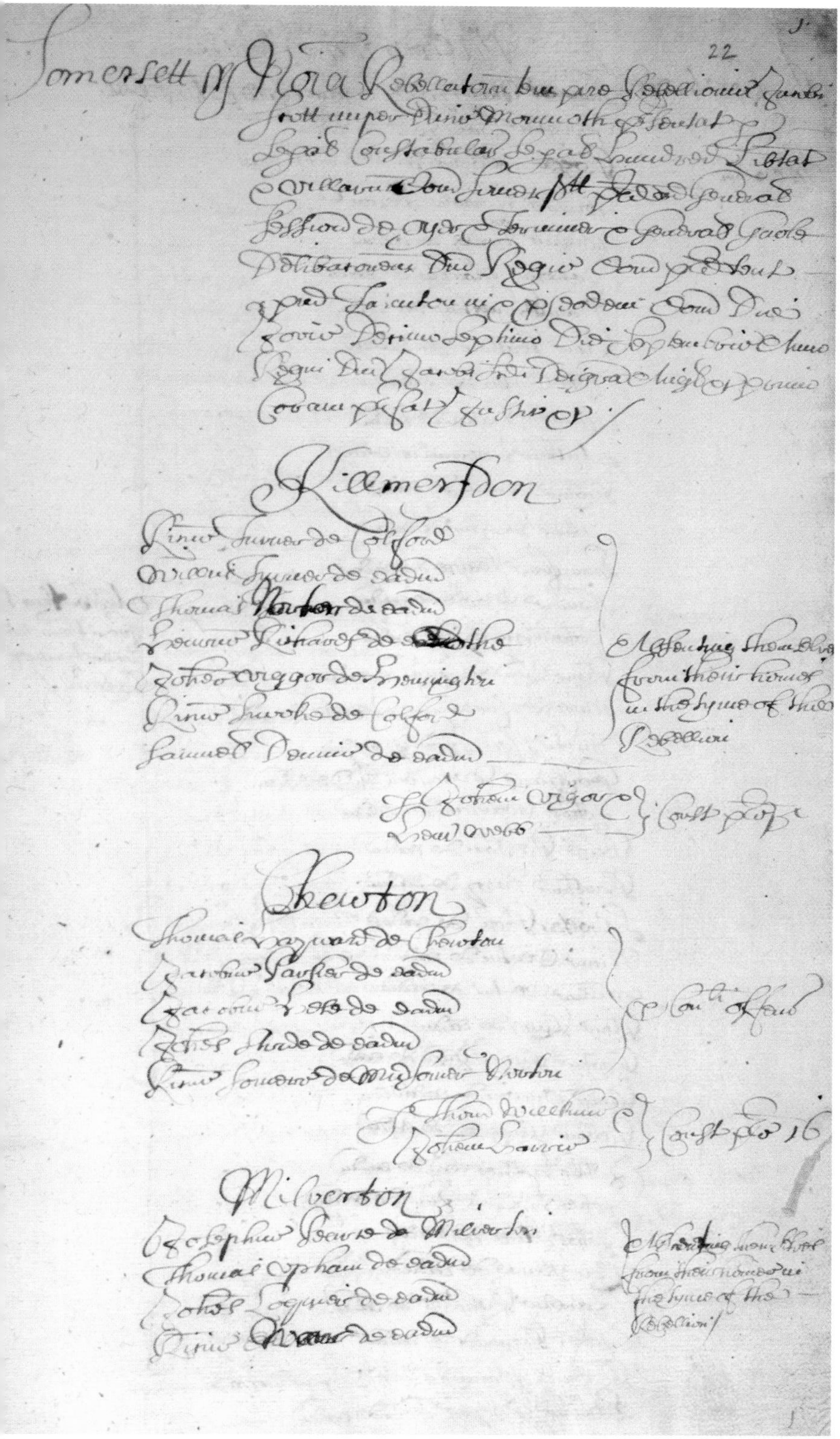

Somersett

22

Kilmersdon

Newton

Milverton

This document, known as the Monmouth Roll, records the fates of those of the Duke's supporters from the Somerset parishes of Kilmersdon, Newtown, and Milverton, who were captured after Sedgemore and taken for trial at Dorchester, in September 1685. These strongly artisan and non-conformist communities provided fertile recruiting grounds for the rebellion, and were consequently singled out for exemplary punishment at the hands of both Judge and King.

If Parliament was willing to pay for James's new soldiers, then it was far from ready to countenance the widespread introduction of Roman Catholic officers into the army, as the King wished. Louis XIV had just withdrawn religious toleration from the French Protestants, with the result that thousands of them were flooding into the British Isles as refugees, recounting their terrible experiences of suffering and intimidation. In such a climate, the fear of many English Protestants that military force would be used to impose Catholicism upon them now acquired a growing currency, as James reached an impasse with his Parliament over the issuing of commissions in contravention of the Test Acts, and prorogued the legislature that – just 10 months earlier – had shown such extraordinary benevolence towards him.

THE BREAK WITH TORY ENGLAND

Thus far James had proved unassailable because of the alliance between the Crown and the supporters of the Anglican Church. Though his own household appears to have remained something of a law unto itself, the King had solid grounds for optimism, if only he could pave the way for a general peace in Europe and avoid being dragged into the escalating conflict between France, on the one hand, and the Dutch together with the German princes, upon the other (see Document 12, *War clouds over Europe*). He had correctly assessed that the outbreak of full-scale war upon the Continent alone could threaten his hold on power and his ambitious legislative programme. Otherwise, his right to sovereignty as a Roman Catholic had been accepted as fact, however grudgingly, by the overwhelming majority of his people. In addition, much could be expected – and even achieved due to the lack of a coherent opposition – through the gradual mitigation of legal restraints upon the types of profession that could be followed by his Catholic subjects. Unfortunately, James was a man in a hurry, who believed that he had been specially chosen by God to aid in the re-establishment of Catholicism across his three kingdoms. Moreover, he was fearful that his eventual successors – who seemed likely to be his daughter, Mary, and her husband William of Orange – would, as Protestants, attempt to undo all of his work. Everything depended, therefore, upon his ability to press on with the removal of all barriers to the advancement of individual Catholics as quickly, and as thoroughly, as possible, in order to make his policies irreversible.

This inevitably began to erode the link between the King and his natural Tory supporters. It became increasingly clear that James was intent on ensuring that members of his own faith had their share of high office, and that he had dedicated himself to destroying any obstacle placed in his path. Having already secured his own appointees at the head of the judiciary, James asserted his right to use the royal prerogative to override – or dispense with – all other legislation. A test case, over the right of Sir Edward Hales – a Roman Catholic officer – to hold a commission, provided the perfect opportunity. In June 1686 the Chief Justice ruled that as 'the laws of England are the king's laws', there was not one single piece of legislation that could not be overturned by the powers of the king. Henceforth, James was effectively above the law. The royal prerogative had been proved to hold greater authority than parliamentary statutes, and legal sanction had been given for the King to begin an all-out assault upon the existing anti-Catholic legislation.

A Commission for Ecclesiastical Causes was appointed by James, in his capacity as head of the Church of England, to act as a royal watchdog, monitoring appointments and removing troublesome clerics – such as Henry Compton, Bishop of London – from their sees. The Commission also assisted in James's plans to open up the universities, which were entirely controlled by the national Church, to Roman Catholic scholars and students. However, while he was able to appoint individual Catholics as masters at Sidney Sussex College, Cambridge, and University College, Oxford, he overreached himself in the case of Magdalen College, Oxford. He decided to impose a candidate as president who was entirely unsuitable for the post on every level, from his academic credentials to his dissolute lifestyle. All that mattered to James was that, as a

12   *War clouds over Europe*

A letter from James to Prince William of Orange, 2 February 1686.

Though James had attempted a thorough-going reform of the life of the court at his accession, cutting down on its expenditure, rationalising its offices and imposing a higher moral tone upon its members, he seemed utterly incapable of controlling the quarrelsome behaviour of his friends. Duels between the members of his household were commonplace. As a young man, John Churchill had fought two spectacularly unsuccessful duels, resulting in his being disarmed and badly cut about, while the Earl of Tyrconnel enjoyed a justifiable reputation for having a quick temper and a willingness to settle his quarrels with the point of his sword. However, the killing of an aristocrat by one of the illegitimate sons of Charles II, over a point of honour, was something that King James simply could not ignore. It was with some difficulty that Grafton, who had distinguished himself in the campaign against Monmouth, was kept out of reach of the courts.

More seriously, the political temperature had been raised in Europe by Louis XIV's forced conversion or expulsion of the French Protestant communities, and by the Duke of Savoy's undertaking to extirpate Protestantism from his own lands. Thrown back upon the defensive, William of Orange was under no illusion that the French were planning another strike against the Dutch Republic, though James would have had him believe otherwise. This letter was written from Whitehall.

THE LETTER READS:

I have had yours of the 5th [New Style], in which you say, somewhere, you are begin[ning] to be alarmed at a voyage the King of France is to make this spring. All that I can say upon it is, that I do not think he will do anything to disturb the peace of Christendom for several reasons, and his ministers here say it also; and I do what I can to let them see the inconveniences that may happen to their master, should he begin a war, and will still do what is in my power to prevent it. As for news, the Duke of Grafton had this morning the misfortune to kill Jack Talbot, the Earl of Shrewsbury's brother. It was Talbot gave the first …

The letter continues:

offence, and sent the challenge, as I am told. The Duke of Grafton is withdrawn, and I have not yet heard what the Coroner's inquest have found.

Whithall Feb: 2: 1686:

I have had yours of the 5: in w:ch you
say, some where you are, begin to be
allarum'd at a voyage, the King of
france is to make this spring, all
that I can say upon it is, that I do
not think he will do any thing to
disturbe the peace of Christendome,
for severall reasons, and his ministers
here say it also, and I do what I can
to lett them see the inconveniences
which may happen to their master
should he begin a war, and will still
do what is in my power to prevent
it, as for newse the D: of Grafton
had this morning, the misfortune
to kill Jack Talbot, the E: of Shrewsburys
Brother, t'was Talbot gave the first

Roman Catholic, Anthony Farmer should have the office. As a result, a traditionally loyal institution was alienated from the monarchy and James was forced to intervene personally, upbraiding the members of the 'stubborn, turbulent college' and expelling all the Fellows who voted against his compromise candidate. He even managed to divide his hand-picked Ecclesiastical Commission over the matter. Having shaken the hold of the Church of England, he prepared to break with his Tory supporters and to cast about for new partners, from outside the established political spectrum, with whom to refashion the State.

RELIGIOUS TOLERATION

James's administration was now entering entirely unfamiliar territory. The majority of his Anglican advisors, including Lord Rochester, had left office and been replaced by an ambitious group of Roman Catholic converts, such as the Earls of Sunderland and Melfort, who had risen fast in the King's service. They were inclined to tell the King exactly what he wished to hear, in stark contrast to members of the older Catholic nobility, who feared that his headlong rush to empower members of their faith would result in disaster for them all.

James, however, had come to the conclusion that once a level playing field had been established between the different religions, his subjects would be bound to discover, just as he had, the true essence of Roman Catholicism and be won over by its arguments. He envisaged a comprehensive form of religious toleration, embracing both Catholic and Protestant dissenters. In the spring of 1687 he therefore used his prerogative to make a Declaration of Indulgence, which benefited all non-Anglicans (see Document 13, *James grants liberty of conscience*).

With letters of support forthcoming from Baptist and Quaker communities, though not, it was noted, from the more numerous Presbyterians, James saw a

1. The King.
2. The Prince of Denmark.
3, 4. The Archbishops of Canterbury and York.
5. The Speaker.

6. The Chancellor with the Great Seal.
7. The Bishops, twenty-five in number.
8. The Dukes and Peers.
9. The Members sitting on Woolsacks.

10. The Barons and Lords of the Kingdom.
11, 12. The Lawyers.
13. The Herald.
14. The Spectators.

possibility to forge an alliance between these disadvantaged Protestant groups and the Roman Catholics. If they could be persuaded to work together under the protection of the Crown, then the Anglican grip on Parliament could be broken and the Test Acts and penal laws permanently repealed. Consequently, by the summer of 1687 James had committed himself to securing the return of a new Parliament, comprising dissenters as well as Anglicans, which was capable of delivering his radical religious reforms. Unfortunately, it would seem that he had seriously underestimated the strength of opposition from the existing political elites, who had done well out of the Restoration Settlement and had no wish to be replaced by a new and largely synthetic ruling class. They were already preparing to fight a bitter rearguard action against the King's innovations in Church and State. Revolution was far from their minds, but James's attempts to centralise power and redraw religious boundaries would seriously test their loyalty and result in the fracturing of the political consensus built up since 1660, turning all of the King's achievements to dust.

King James convenes a sitting of the House of Lords, while Lord North – soon to be replaced as Chancellor by Judge Jeffreys – displays the Great Seal. Despite the heavy electoral defeat of the Whigs in the Commons, and the continuing goodwill of the peers, James would squander all-too quickly the Parliamentary support for his regime.

A letter from James to Prince William of Orange, 18 March 1687.

At the Restoration, James had strongly opposed toleration for Protestant dissenters, equating them with republicanism and advocating stern measures to limit the spread of Quakerism and the activities of ejected ministers. However, after his own conversion, he came increasingly to experience religious persecution first hand. He began to realise that his own position as a member of a minority faith was analogous to that of other individuals forced into opposition to the monarchy simply on account of their personal faith. His burgeoning friendship with William Penn the younger led him to understand and respect the Quakers, while the realisation that both Protestant dissenters and Roman Catholics were increasingly involving themselves in business and foreign trade led him to appreciate that religious freedom could act as a stimulus to economic growth.

Moreover, having been converted to the Catholic Church primarily on an intellectual, rather than an emotional, level, James prided himself upon his own powers of reasoning. He believed that if all religious arguments were presented fairly, then an individual could not fail to be convinced by Catholicism in exactly the same manner that he had been. In this light, there was simply no need for intimidation or coercion. All that was needed was an open mind and an atmosphere of general religious toleration in which debate could flourish. Unfortunately, Louis XIV's brutal destruction of French Protestantism after 1685 coincided with James's rule and tended to reinforce in England the widespread identification of Catholicism as an alien and persecuting creed. Worse still, James's own attempts at proselytising were either curiously ham-fisted or spectacularly ill-judged, leading him to promote the incompetent, such as Anthony Farmer, or to favour disproportionately those, such as Sunderland and Melfort, whose conversions spoke of nothing save expediency and a desire to further their careers. It is impossible to judge whether James might eventually have turned to force, as opposed to bribery, to further the reconversion of England, but it stands to his credit that he appears to have genuinely believed in the necessity for toleration and refused to abandon his principles during the years of his final exile. This letter was written from Whitehall.

THE LETTER READS:

I had yours of the 21st [New Style] from The Hague, so late on Tuesday last, that I could not then let you know I had received it. I see by it that you were satisfied that the peace of Christendom would be preserved at least for this year. I am of your opinion, too, and you know was all along of [the] opinion that France would be quiet, believing it [was] not their interest to be otherwise. I have this day resolved to prorogue the Parliament till the 22nd November next, and that all my subjects may be at ease and quiet, and mind their trades and private concerns, have resolved to give liberty of conscience to all Dissenters whatsoever, having been ever against persecuting any for conscience sake. I have not time to say more but that you shall always find me as kind to you as you can desire.

Whitehall Mar: 18: 1687.   30

I had yours of the 21: from the Hage, so
late on tuesday last, that I could not than
lett you know I had received it, I see by
it you were satisfyd that the peace of
Christendome would be preserved at least
for this yeare, I am of your opinion to
and you know, was all along of opinion
that france would be quiet beleuing
it not their interest to be otherwise;
I have this day resolved to prorogue
the Parliament till the 22: of Nou:
next; and that all my subjects may
be at ease, and quiet, and mind their
trads, and privat concerns, have resolved
to give liberty of concience to all dissenters
what so ever, haueing been euer against
persecuting any for concience sake, I
haue not tyme to say more but that
you shall always find me as kind to you
as you can desire. ₰. 58

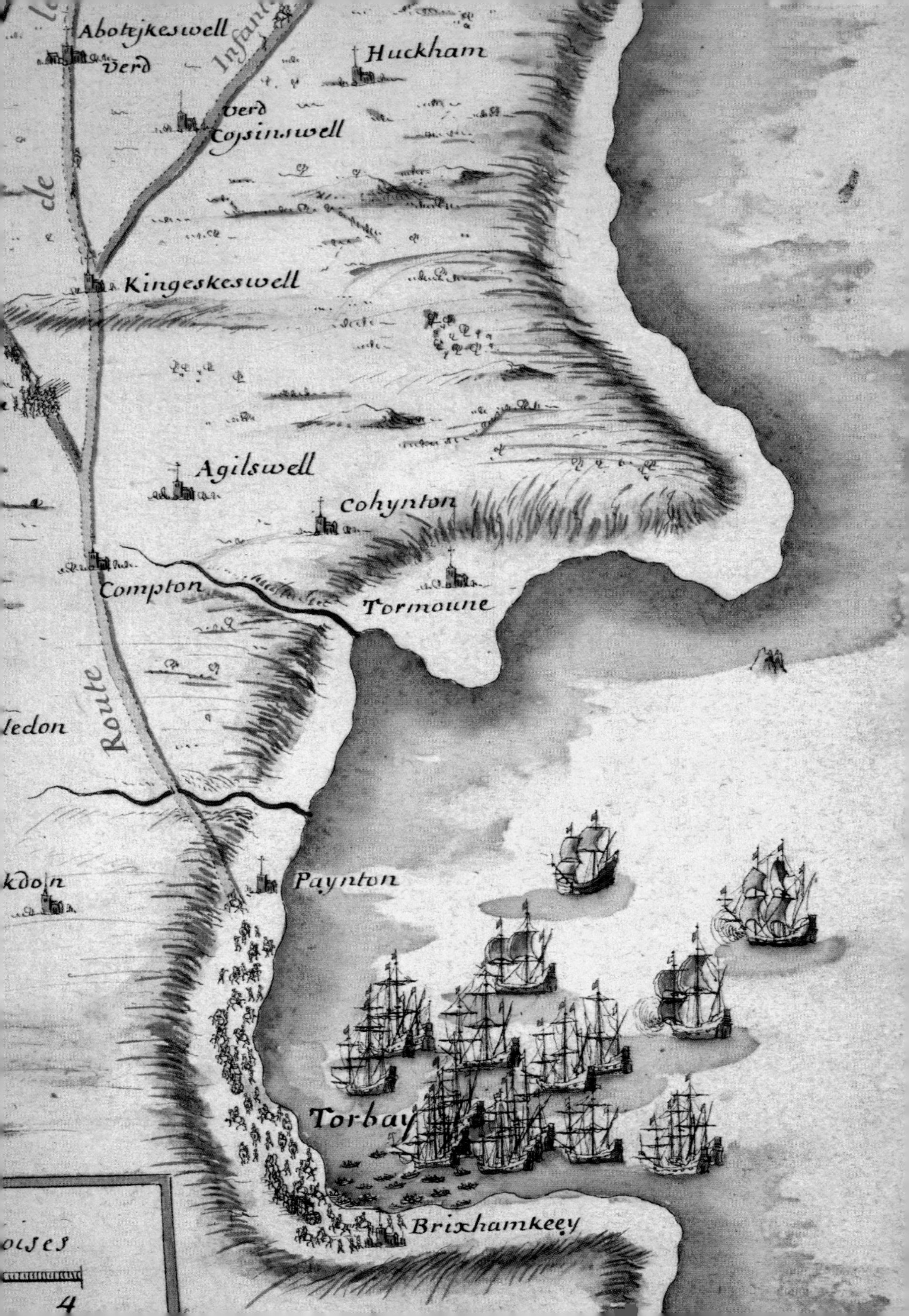
Abotejkeswell
Verd
Infant
Huckham
Verd
Cosinswell
de
Kingeskeswell
Agilswell
Cohynton
Compton
Tormoune
Route
ledon
Paynton
kdon
Torbay
Brixhamkeey
oises
4

The Collapse of a Regime

ATTACK UPON LOCAL GOVERNMENT
AND THE ESTABLISHED CHURCH

I n order to ensure that his own candidates would be elected to
Parliament, James began to reorganise local government and
conducted an election tour. He swept through the south west
of England, Wales and the Midlands in an attempt to harness the
support of the rural gentry.

The administration of the counties was overhauled. Appointees
loyal to the Crown were created lord lieutenants of Lancashire,
Shropshire and Warwickshire, in place of their traditional aristocratic incumbents. Anglican Justices of the Peace were purged in
favour of Catholic and Protestant dissenters, and the borough
charters were rewritten in order to favour parliamentary candidates
who had the King's backing.

A contemporary French
map depicts the landing
of Prince William's army
at Torbay and the route he
took inland, to the village
of Abbotskerswell, with his
cavalry escort, while his
infantry drove on towards
Exeter by a parallel road.
Initially the locals – shown
here crowding the sands –
came to look and to cheer,
but did not flock to join
his colours.

In Ireland James's friend and confidant the Earl of Tyrconnel
had risen to control both the army and the civil administration. He
recruited large numbers of Catholic soldiers, displacing Protestant
officers and officials, and appointed his co-religionists to key
positions in the military and the government. Though James had
never stopped believing in the necessity of having a strong army,
and Tyrconnel saw these measures as doing no more than redress-
ing long-standing grievances felt by Irish Catholics, such rapid
developments chilled the blood of Protestant Englishmen. They
feared for their security now that this seemingly unstoppable
military force could be quickly and easily deployed against them.

THE SEVEN BISHOPS AND THE PRINCE OF WALES

James now sought to press home his advantage by issuing a Second Declaration of Indulgence in April 1688, guaranteeing all religions the right to worship as they pleased. However, in a startling display of tactlessness, he ordered that the Declaration should be read out from every Anglican pulpit. This proved to be one step too far for the clergy of the Church of England, who were being asked to participate in the dismemberment of their own institution. Though none were natural rebels, seven Anglican bishops – led by the Archbishop of Canterbury – presented a petition to the King outlining their reasons for refusing to read the text in church and disputing the validity of the dispensing power. Enraged, James ordered their arrest and had them conveyed to the Tower of London to await their trial for treason.

Having alienated the majority of his original followers and managed to unite the political nation in opposition to his policies, by

This Dutch engraving shows the seven bishops being rowed, under heavy guard, towards Traitors' Gate and their confinement in the Tower of London. Though barges crammed full of well-wishers cheered them on, few could have expected the collapse of the case against them and their triumphant acquittal.

the summer of 1688 James found himself in an unexpectedly precarious position. His new alliances with the Catholics and Protestant dissenters were fragile and largely untested, while the birth of his son in June opened up the issue of the succession once more (see Document 14, *The birth of the Prince of Wales*).

The birth of a son and heir to James, celebrated by this medallion appeared nothing short of miraculous to his supporters and deeply suspicious to his foes. The privacy of the Queen's confinement aroused suspicion, and even James's own daughter, Anne, affected to believe that her new step-brother was no more than an impostor, to be foisted upon the Protestant nation by the Catholics at court.

Besieged by a hostile mob, the King's judges deliberated in Westminster Hall over the evidence brought against the seven bishops. Amid jeers and catcalls, two of the four judges recommended that the accused should be convicted, but their remaining colleagues – whether through conviction or fear of the consequences – broke ranks and directed that the jury should acquit. Last-minute attempts at intimidation by the King's supporters failed, and the jurors returned a verdict of 'not guilty'. To James's dismay, the cheers of the crowds who accompanied the victorious bishops back through London were taken up by his own soldiers encamped on Hounslow Heath.

In hindsight, the writing may already have been upon the wall; James had forfeited the trust and affection of the overwhelming majority of his subjects. Yet the fear of renewed civil war, the lack of an organised opposition and the evident futility of isolated risings – as demonstrated by the fate of Monmouth – all combined to ensure that the country did not stir against him.

However, a catalyst for action was provided by a mixed group of seven Whig and Tory magnates, including Bishop Compton, Admiral Russell and Lord Danby. They wrote to William of Orange imploring him to intervene directly in English affairs, to come over and 'rescue the nation' before the rule of law and the Protestant religion were utterly destroyed. William, who followed English politics closely, had been greatly disturbed by recent events. He realised that if he did not act decisively, his chances of safeguarding his wife's

The birth of the Prince of Wales

A letter from James to Prince William of Orange, 12 June 1688.

Mary of Modena had given birth to four children before the summer of 1688, but all – save for a daughter who did not threaten to alter the succession and died before her 5th birthday – had lived for only a matter of days. With James now in middle age and his wife approaching her thirties, it was widely assumed that they would have no more children and that Princess Mary would succeed to the throne in due course. This knowledge provided a useful safety valve for both English and Dutch politics, creating the impression that James's religious policies would be reversible on the accession of his Protestant daughter and reassuring William of Orange that his wife's inheritance would serve as a bulwark against the encroaching power of France. However, all these illusions were shattered by the birth of a healthy son to the King and Queen, who now took precedence in the succession and raised the spectre of the establishment of a Roman Catholic dynasty, dedicated to forwarding a rolling programme of legislation in favour of their co-religionists.

The news of the birth of an heir was greeted with widespread incredulity. It was quickly – but entirely falsely – held to have been the work of the Jesuit Order, who had smuggled an impostor, the son of a Welsh miller, into the royal apartments in a warming pan and exchanged him for the corpse of the true but stillborn infant. James's joy in his son was entirely unfeigned, but the peace in Western Europe, the victories in the East against the Turks and the division of the French fleet in order to combat pirates, which he cheerfully related in this letter written from St James's Palace, also afforded Prince William a window of opportunity to organise his own forces and to attempt to salvage his own claim to an interest in English affairs.

THE LETTER READS:

The Queen was, God be thanked, safely delivered of a son on Sunday morning, a little before ten. She has been very well ever since, but the child was somewhat ill this last night of the wind and some gripes, but is now, blessed be God, very well again, and like to have no returns of it, and is a very strong boy. Last night I received yours of the 18th [New Style], and hope by this the campaign is well begun towards Belgrade. I expect every day to hear what the French fleet has done at Algiers, having heard they were just arrived before that place. It is late and I have not time to say more but that you shall find me to be as kind to you as you can expect.

St James's June 12: 1688:

The Queene was God be thanked safly
deliverd of a Sonne, on Sonday morning,
a little before ten, she has been very well
ever since, but the Child was somewhat
ill this last night of wind and some
gripe, but is now blessed be God very well
againe, and like to have no returns ont,
and is a very strong boy, last night I
receved yours of the 18: and hope by this
the Campagne is well begun towards Belgrade,
I expect every day to heare what the french
fleett has done at Algers, having heard
they were just arrived before that place,
tis late and I have not tyme to say more
but that you shall find me to be as kind to
you as you can expect. I.

claim to the throne, and of preventing a future military alliance between France and England, would be irretrievably lost. With the support of the States General of Holland, he pulled his army back from the frontier and hastily assembled an invasion fleet, ready for the descent upon England. Unfortunately, even though James was kept fully informed of these extremely worrying developments by his spies and diplomats, he chose to discount their seriousness and limited himself to a perfunctory strengthening of his defences (see Document 15, *A last letter to Prince William*). This abiding sense of hubris was to ensure that James was completely taken by surprise at the news of his nephew's landing and was largely unprepared to stake everything in a fight to the finish in order to preserve his throne, before winter set in.

Though best known for his Diary, Samuel Pepys (1633–1703) was an exemplary civil servant, who quickly mastered naval affairs and devoted himself to the more efficient administration of the service. He remained loyal to his master, King James, at the Revolution and was deprived of his offices. During his enforced, but largely comfortable, retirement, he compiled his history of the Royal Navy, in which he placed himself and James unashamedly centre stage. This portrait is from Colburn's *Memoirs of Samuel Pepys* (1825).

INVASION AND FLIGHT

Storms and bad weather had threatened to disperse William's fleet and held up its departure for more than a week. Yet when it finally put to sea, the English ships sent to intercept it remained inactive, despite all of Samuel Pepys' orders and increasingly shrill injunctions. William was able to land at Torbay on 5 November 1688 entirely unmolested.

James had expected that the invasion would be accompanied by a rising in Yorkshire; now wrong-footed and thoroughly confused by events, he wasted time in recalling the troops he had sent north and in attempting to conciliate his domestic critics. Finally, he determined to confront William and sent his formidable army westwards, under Lord Feversham, establishing a forward base upon Salisbury Plain, in order to bar his further advance. Although the Dutch had been able to gain entry to Exeter, the regional centre, few English recruits and only a handful of the gentry had joined them. In fact, William had begun seriously to consider the possibility of abandoning the campaign and returning with his army to Holland.

In the meantime, James had joined his troops upon Salisbury Plain, intending to force a decisive battle and to lead his regiments in person. However, it was here that disaster overtook him. Instead of immediately marching towards William's scouts at Axminster, he dithered about camp, incapacitated by nosebleeds and haunted by fears of treachery (see Document 16, *The collapse on Salisbury Plain*). In the absence of strong leadership, a trickle of desertions began to turn into a flood, and after five days James ordered a retreat to London. Leaving his soldiers to their fate (see Document 17, *The royal army is disbanded*), he rushed back to the capital, only to find that his daughter – Anne – had abandoned him and that risings against him had flared across the north and the Midlands.

Pepys was well aware that the English fleet should have intercepted the Dutch invasion force and desperately attempted to compel individual captains to draw together as they sheltered, inactive, in port. What he did not realise was the level of disaffection in the navy. The senior officers had already determined to ignore his orders.

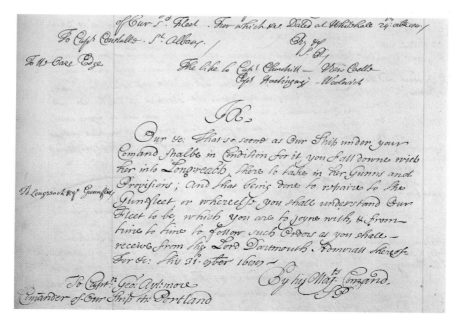

15 *A last letter to Prince William*

A letter from James to Prince William of Orange, 17 September 1688.

James knew full well that William was in contact with the English opposition. He was also aware of both his negotiations for men and money from the German princes and the possibility that his mustering of troops at Nijmegen was no more than a diversion, calculated to deflect attention away from his invasion of England. Therefore, while preserving the diplomatic niceties in his correspondence with his nephew, his words carried with them an implicit threat. He had learned the lessons of the Dutch raid upon the royal dockyards in 1667. If William's ships should be sent once again up the Thames and Medway, then his new gun emplacements would be ready and waiting to receive them. However, despite all the evidence to the contrary and the stern warnings of Louis XIV, James still refused to acknowledge the imminence of the danger posed to him by William and had no way of knowing that this letter, for his 'Son the Prince of Orange', written from Windsor Castle, was to be the last that he would ever send him.

THE LETTER READS:

I have received yours of the 17th [New Style] from The Hague, by which I find you were come back thither from a voyage you had made into Germany, to speak with some of the Princes there. I was very glad to hear, by an express which came to the Spanish ambassador here, of the taking of Belgrade, which, with the taking of Gradiska [Gradeska-Planina in modern-day Macedonia], will secure the Emperor's conquests in those parts. I am sorry there is so much likelihood of war upon the Rhine, nobody wishing more the peace of Christendom than myself. I intend to go tomorrow to London, and the next day to Chatham, to see the condition of the new batteries I have made in the Medway, and my ships which are there. The Queen and my son are to be at London on Thursday, which is all I shall say, but that you shall find me as kind to you as you can expect.

Windsor Sep: 18. 1688: 102

I have received yours of the 17: from the
Hage, by w:ch I find you were come back
thether from a voyage you had made
into Germany to speake with some of
the Princes there, I was very glad to
heare by an expresse w:ch came to the
Spanish Embassador here of the takeing
of Belgrade, w:ch with the takeing of Gradiska
will secure the Emperors conquests in those
parts, I am sorry there is so much likelyhood
of war upon the Rheyn no body wishing
more the peace of Christendome then
my self, I intend to go tomorrow to London
and the next day to Chatham to see
the condition of the new batterys I have
made in the Medway and my Ships w:ch
are there, the Queene and my Sonne are
to be at London on thursday, w:ch is all I shall
say, but that you shall find me as kind to
you as you can expect.

The collapse on Salisbury Plain

A letter from the Earl of Middleton to Lord Preston, 24 November 1688.

To begin with, James had appeared to be in a very strong position against William's invasion force. The appetite of the West Country for further rebellion had been largely destroyed by Judge Jeffreys' brutal application of the law some three years earlier. Consequently, the overwhelming majority of the population now maintained a wary sense of neutrality until they could be sure that William was not about to turn tail and flee back to Holland, leaving them just as swiftly as he had come and abandoning them to the doubtful mercy of the King and his Lord Chancellor. Indeed, some twenty-five thousand men of the new royal army were concentrated about Salisbury when James rode into camp on 19 November 1688, with a further seven thousand marching to join them and the same number held in reserve to guard the capital. Yet the King hesitated to strike at his foes and occupied his time conducting pointless reviews and inspections, fulfilling the role but not the function of a general. Having never before held independent command of an army, he had no clear grasp of how best to proceed and was seized by crippling indecision, even as his officers were beginning to consider how to secure their own futures without him. With Feversham seemingly unaware of the exact location of his enemy and unwilling to send out scouting parties, lest they desert, James was even abandoned by John Churchill, who owed him everything and had been his favourite servant.

The Earl of Middleton, writing to Lord Preston from Salisbury on 24 November 1688, gave vent to his anxiety and the atmosphere of mutual suspicion that prevailed in the royal camp as the fabric of James's beloved army began to dissolve.

THE LETTER READS:

I have received yours of the 22nd this morning. Roger Huett brought news from Warminster that Lord Churchill's Grenadiers went last night over to the enemy; that Maine was gone in pursuit of them but is suspected to have gone after them. The Duke of Grafton and Lord Churchill are missing, and not doubted but they are gone to the enemy. They went from hence. We have had no advice from Warminster but what Huett brought, which would make one imagine that the whole brigade is gone, commanded by Kirke and Trelawny. It was lucky that the King's bleeding at the nose hindered him from going thither, where they might have seized him. He marches this day to Wallop with all his troops, and so by Andover to London.

My Lord:

To Preston.   I have recd yor Lops of ye 22th this morning
Roger Huett brought News from Warminster,
yt Lord Churchill's Grenadiers went last night
over to ye Enemy, yt Maine was gone in
pursuit of them, but is suspected to have gone
after them, ye D. of Grafton & Lord Churchill
are missing, & not doubted but they are gone
after them into ye Enemy, these two last
went from hence. Wee have had no
advice from Warminster but what R. Huett
brought wch would make one imagine yt ye
whole Brigade is gone, commanded by Kirke
& Trelawny, it was lucky yt ye King's bleeding
at ye nose hindred him from going thither,
where they might have seized his sacred
Person, wch God long pserve. The King
marches this day to Wallop wth all his Troops,
& so by Andover to London. I am

My Lord

Yor most faithfull
humble servant

Middleton,

17   *The royal army is disbanded*

A letter from the Earl of Feversham to Prince William of Orange, 11 December 1688.

On the road back to London, James's army lost the last of its fragile cohesion. Driven relentlessly eastwards by the advancing Dutch, men slipped away, officers joined the opposing camp and units became hopelessly intermingled. With winter setting in and food and forage growing scarce, several thousand soldiers halted in the fields that stretched from Windsor to Uxbridge and awaited their uncertain fate. Among the private soldiers and non-commissioned officers there was a sense of residual loyalty to their King, but neither the will nor the leadership existed to turn it to good account. As James prepared to flee to France, he wrote to his army commander thanking him for his loyalty and that of his troops, but commended them not to 'expose yourselves by resisting a foreign army'. Feversham read the letter out loud to his men, many of whom broke down in tears when they heard its contents and learned of the depths of the King's despair. Feversham then communicated his desire to avoid further bloodshed to the Prince of Orange in this letter written from Uxbridge. Unfortunately, rather than waiting for instructions from William, Feversham interpreted his last instructions from the King as meaning that he should disband his army forthwith. The result was that thousands of leaderless, hungry and unpaid troops fanned out across the countryside, and bands of Irish soldiers headed north, desperate to obtain their passage home. As James's grand army ceased to exist, William had Feversham arrested for his incompetence and sent Churchill and Grafton to round up the shattered units and to attempt to reimpose some form of order upon them.

THE LETTER READS:

Having received this morning a letter from his Majesty with the unfortunate news of his resolution to go out of England, and that he is actually gone, I thought myself obliged, being at the head of his army, having received his Majesty's order to make no opposition against anybody, to let your ...

The letter continues:

Highness know it, with the advice of all the officers that are here, as soon as it was possible to hinder the misfortune of effusion of blood. I have sent order already to that purpose to all the troops that are under my command, which shall be the last order they shall receive from, Sir, your Highness' most humble and obedient servant.

N

having received this morning
a letter from his maiesty, with
the enfortunate news of his
resolution to goe out of england,
and that he is actually gone,
I thought my selfe oblidged
being att the head of his army,
having received his maiestys
order to make no opposition
againkt any body. to lett your

In a last, desperate attempt to cling on to his throne, he attempted to open negotiations with William. He promised that he would overturn the policies of the last two years and agreed to the summoning of a fresh Parliament, elected without undue interference by the Crown. Though overdue, such concessions might have yielded results and have served to rally the King's Tory supporters to his side. However, James's terror of capture – and the disgrace and possible trial that might have accompanied it – gained complete mastery over him. Without word to his followers, on 12 December 1688 he burned the writs issued for the general election and escaped across the Thames, casting the Great Seal into the river as he went.

Unfortunately, despite his disguise, James was apprehended by a gang of Kentish fishermen who, believing that they had caught a 'hatchet-faced Jesuit', cuffed him about the face and rifled through his pockets. It was only with some difficulty that the King was rescued from their clutches and returned to London with an escort of cavalry. This was the last thing that William of Orange wanted; James's continued presence threatened to break the remarkable

This Victorian oil painting, by E.M. Ward, evokes the sense of corruption and malaise that gripped both the king and his council, upon the approach of their enemy. While the courtiers continue with their frivolities, and the little Prince of Wales plays with his nurses, his father's power begins to unravel, from its heart, in the palace of Whitehall. Devastated by the news of his nephew's landing, James lets the crucial despatch fall from his grasp and slumps, insensible, in his chair. Though the Queen rushes to his aid, his priests do nothing to help him, while a nobleman eavesdrops from behind a screen and prepares to slip past the guards, to go to William with word of the collapse of the King's resolve.

political consensus that had joyfully welcomed his slow advance upon the capital and which, since the debacle at Salisbury Plain, had looked to him to settle the future governance of the nation. Moreover, the problem of what was actually to be done with the King now presented itself. In his misfortune, he appeared a far more sympathetic figure than had ever previously been the case. There was no desire to deprive him of his life or necessarily even to strip him of his crown. What was popularly demanded was a limitation of his powers and a guarantee that a Protestant should succeed him after his death, and that Prince William should be accorded an executive role in the formulation of policy and the control of the armed forces.

Yet James was fundamentally opposed to any limitations being placed upon his prerogative and, though he led his followers to believe the contrary, he had set his face against further negotiations. Instead, on 23 December he mounted a second escape attempt that, this time, proved successful. William, who had known and even ensured that the back door to the King's residence remained unguarded, was extremely relieved to see him gone. James, however, believed that by leaving for France he would throw the nation into unprecedented administrative chaos, that the State would be unable to function without him, and that his subjects would soon be forced to welcome his swift recall. Unfortunately for him, he had seriously underestimated both the political skills of Prince William and the creativity, pragmatism and independence of those he had once ruled.

At Hungerford, James's commissioners met with William of Orange and attempted to negotiate a blueprint for a future government, and a timetable for fresh elections to a free Parliament. The Prince's terms were not excessive or severe, but each of the commissioners shifted for himself, wasted precious time, and failed to report back accurately to the King, their master. Frightened and confused by these developments, James resolved to abandon the negotiations and flee into exile.

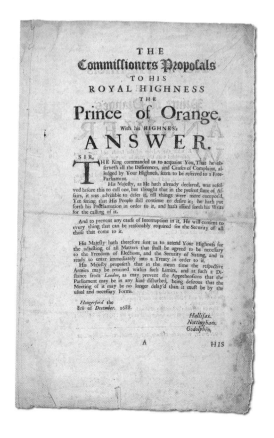

The Fallen King

JAMES IN IRELAND

Once in France, James was graciously received by Louis XIV and reunited with his wife and child. Anxious to prosecute his war against the Dutch and to restore James to his throne, Louis wasted no time in equipping an expedition to carry the fallen King to Ireland, where Tyrconnel was still holding out in his name.

In the meantime, the English Parliament called in James's absence had decided to view the King's flight as an abdication and declared that he had wilfully left the throne vacant. After much dispute, a compromise was reached whereby William and Mary were offered the Crown as joint sovereigns, and a Declaration of Rights was passed into law that proved a damning indictment of James's reign. He was viewed as a man for arbitrary power, a cruel and unjust king whose actions had necessitated the curtailment of the royal prerogative and the equitable – and, as it turned out, extremely durable – rebalancing of powers between Crown and Parliament (see Document 18, *James's statue is pulled down*).

Though the King's remaining Tory supporters fought a desperate rearguard action, in both the Commons and the Lords, to preserve his authority, James failed to provide them with clear advice and devoted himself instead to pursuing a military – rather than a political – solution to his problems. In March 1689 he landed in Ireland and was afforded a hero's welcome when he entered Dublin on Palm Sunday. He quickly established the jurisdiction of his government right across the land, save for a handful of pockets

Though small, stooping and asthmatic, William III was brave, intelligent and an extremely skilled politician. He proved a dutiful and extremely capable monarch, though his dour nature and foreign accent ensured that he commanded respect rather than affection from his British subjects. He was devastated by the death of his wife, in 1694, but managed to confound a series of Jacobite plots and assassination attempts, while doing much to strengthen the administrative and financial systems of both Great Britain and Holland. Exhausted by his labours, he died after laying the foundations of a Grand Alliance of European powers, capable of successfully combating Louis XIV's aggressions. Oil painting after Sir Godfrey Kneller.

The testimony of Thomas Mortimer before the Mayor of Newcastle-upon-Tyne, 23 May 1689.

It is often falsely argued that the events of 1688-9 did not constitute a revolution but were only part of a palace coup that ultimately changed little in the governance of the kingdom. However, the collapse of James II's power was as total as it was devastatingly swift. Riots broke out against him in London, and popular risings convulsed the north and the Midlands. Nor did passions subside quickly. In Newcastle-upon-Tyne, the garrison, groups of sailors and the Whig townsfolk were soon to be pitched against their Tory neighbours and the city authorities over the fate of the region's most famous landmark.

Sir William Cleagh, the Mayor in 1685, had raised an enormous brass statue of James on horseback at the quayside in Newcastle, lavishing money and superb craftsmanship on the figure and the depictions of his military triumphs carved on its marble plinth. Unfortunately, at the Revolution it became the most visible symbol of the discredited regime and, on the night of 11 May 1689, a band of soldiers took matters into their own hands. While a crowd assembled on the quayside to listen to speeches, the soldiers toured the local coffee shops announcing their intention to pull down the offending statue. Captain Killigrew, operating under orders from his colonel, raised the temper of the mob to fever pitch, inciting them against their former king and distributing coins among the populace, telling them that unlike James he came to give them money and not to take it from them. As soldiers hacked off the figure's stirrups and spurs, a noose was thrown about its neck and the crowd pulled it tight, eventually dislodging the brass rider from his mount and sending him spinning down into the dust. It was then that the mob closed in upon it, beating the image of James with stones and seeing off a handful of observers who objected to the destruction of a work of art and an expression of civic pride.

Finally, the figure of the horse was dismantled and thrown into the River Tyne, together with the dismembered limbs and the head of the rider, while the crowd gouged chunks of marble out of the empty pedestal. Enraged at the breakdown of law and order and the inflammatory role of the soldiers in channelling an otherwise spontaneous and peaceful protest, the city authorities collected evidence about the disturbances and forwarded them to Lord Danby for consideration by the government in London. However, the State needed loyal and active soldiers, and no action was taken against Captain Killigrew and his men.

Thomas Mortimer, gentleman, gave this evidence about the disturbances before Nicholas Ridley, the Mayor of Newcastle-upon-Tyne, on 23 May 1689.

MORTIMER'S EVIDENCE READS:

Deposes that his being on the Sandhill on Saturday the eleventh instant, about nine at night, and seeing an officer upon the mountebank stage (who as he was told was Captain Killigrew) making speeches to the people. He drew near and heard him say, 'our laws, liberties, and properties were taken away, and by that picture [i.e. the figure of James II]' pointing to it, and then threw money among the people. Soon after he saw a man in a red coat (who he believed was a soldier) pull a rope about the neck of the picture, after which it was pulled down and that he likewise saw several soldiers, with their carbines, among the people near the statue at the same time that the picture was pulled down.

Deposeth that he being on the Sandhill on Saturday the Eleventh
Instant about nine at night & seeing an officer upon the
mountebank stage (who as he was told was Cap.ᵗ
Killigrew) making Speeches to the people he drew near
& heard him say, our Laws liberties & properties
were taken away, & all by that picture pointing to it,
& then threw money among the people soon after
he see a man in a red coat (who he believes was
a Souldier) put a rope about the neck of the picture
after w.ᵗʰ it was pulled down, and that he likewise
see severall Souldiers with their carbines among
the people near the Statue at the same time that
the picture was pulled down.

Capᵗ & Jurat Cord me.

Niᶜ Ridley Major   Tho. Mortimer

127

of resistance in the Protestant enclaves of the north. Unfortunately, his attempts to subdue the fortress city of Derry failed. He was forced to commit the bulk of his army to a long, and ultimately unrewarding, siege rather than immediately crossing with them into Scotland, as he had originally hoped.

The proclamation of King William and Queen Mary by the Scottish Parliament in April 1689 had not been uniformly welcomed across the northern kingdom. John Graham of Claverhouse attempted to raise the clans of the Great Glen in James's name. He managed to rout the government army sent against him in a costly encounter at the Pass of Killiecrankie in July 1689, but he was mortally wounded at the moment of victory. His Highlanders advanced upon Perth but met with stubborn resistance from the Lowland Cameronian Regiment, entrenched behind the walls of Dunkeld. In the subsequent battle, repeated charges by the clansmen were shot down in the town's narrow lanes. The shattered remnants of their army drew off under the cover of darkness, effectively bringing the first Jacobite rebellion to an end.

Possessing more artillery than the Jacobites, William's army was quickly able to beat their foes back from the banks of the Boyne and to silence their heavy guns, so that the English, Dutch, Danish, and Huguenot could storm across the river line and seize the strategic village of Oldbridge.

Victoire Remportée par Le Roy Guillaume III. sur les Irlandoise a la Ruuere de Boyne en Irlande le 3 Juillet 1690.
Designé apres la Nature et paint pour le Roy et Gravé par Theodor Maas.

At the climax of the fight for Oldbridge, Marshal Schomberg was surrounded and shot down. His lifeless body is shown being carried from the field, in this much later engraving by Grainger (1790), as William calmly takes control of the situation, rallying his troops and charging home into the heart of his foes.

While the fighting was still raging in Scotland, William had taken steps to root James out of his base in Ireland. He despatched a mixed force of British, Dutch, Huguenot and German regiments across the Irish Sea, under the command of the elderly Marshal Schomberg. However, their advance was painfully slow, as James simply retreated before them, and Schomberg's soldiers were ravaged by disease and the cold and wet of an Irish winter. In the following summer, William determined to take matters into his own hands, landing in Ireland and ordering an immediate advance upon Dublin. In an attempt to save his capital, on 1 July 1690 James turned and made a stand on the River Boyne. The resulting battle was a disaster, as James allowed his forces to become divided and then fled the fighting precipitately, as his foes stormed his makeshift defences on the south bank. Even though Tyrconnel was able to prolong the war for a further year, James decided to abandon his loyal Irish allies and fled back to France.

THE PENSIONER OF THE KING OF FRANCE

A coach speeds towards the formal gardens and terraces of the Chateau-Neuf at St Germain-en-Laye in a contemporary painting by Adam Frans van der Meulen. James spent the last decade of his life here, together with his court of squabbling and increasingly disappointed followers, in circumstances of great comfort and some opulence.

Hopes of James's restoration were not immediately abandoned. With French backing, fresh invasion fleets were assembled to carry James back home. However, English raiding parties burned his ships down to the waterline at the battle of La Hogue in 1692, while he watched helplessly from the cliffs. Four years later his forces were broken up when an expected rising in England, timed to coincide with their landing, failed to materialise.

Attempts to overthrow William III now took on a far more desperate and conspiratorial character, with a plot to assassinate the King failing in 1696, and James – apparently – being prepared to countenance further attacks on his rival throughout his time in exile (see Document 19, *An assassination plot*).

With Louis XIV furnishing him with a generous pension and the use of the Chateau of St Germain-en-Laye outside Paris, James was able to establish a little court and to oversee both the maintenance of etiquette and the education of his young children. Yet, as the French and Allied armies fought each other to a standstill in Flanders, James's position became more precarious. Clamouring for bread and an end to a war fought for his advantage, mobs protested outside the walls of his palace and stoned his guards. Worse still, James's representatives were excluded from the peace talks held at Ryswick, and Louis XIV began to look for an honourable means of extricating himself from his seemingly limitless commitment to his unfortunate, and increasingly unwelcome, guest.

The death of the King of Poland appeared to offer him just such an opportunity. The Polish Crown was elective and, with the correct bribes to the Polish nobility, Louis was convinced that he could ensure James's successful elevation. The plan had much to recommend it. At a stroke, it would restore James to his former dignity – though in Poland rather than in England – it would reassure the English and the Dutch of France's commitment to peace, and it would guarantee Louis a loyal client in the east. Unfortunately, James fought hard against the suggestion. His conception of his own kingship was profoundly English: he had a God-given right to his father's thrones but not to those of foreign lands, and there the matter was allowed to rest.

With the conclusion of the Peace of Ryswick in September 1697, James lost much of his remaining political influence and the control of his Irish regiments, which were transferred to the French army and formed the famous 'Wild Geese' battalions. As many of his followers began quietly to take their leave of St Germain and attempted to come to terms with the Williamite government, so that they might be allowed to return home, James found himself and his cause increasingly marginalised. He turned to his faith for solace and an explanation of his sad predicament.

An assassination plot

The testimony given to the English Privy Council by William Butler, a Jacobite turned informant, 11 November 1701.

While it seems unlikely that James actually initiated the plans to murder his nephew, there is reason to suspect that he was not averse to the idea of assassination in order to further his aims, provided that he was not implicated in the act and stood at least at one remove from it. As a young man he had been prepared to sanction the killing of Oliver Cromwell, and he had shown little compunction in training his guns directly on William III at the Battle of the Boyne. As a result, while the assassination plots of the 1690s sprang spontaneously from the anger and disappointment felt by many of his former soldiers, his protestations of innocence soon began to wear perilously thin. Consequently, when repeated rumours reached both the Privy Council in Whitehall and the English Embassy in Paris that a new air-gun prototype had been developed by the Jacobite exiles specifically to kill William silently, they were taken extremely seriously indeed.

Though the evidence of a paid informer such as William Butler may have been coloured to reflect popular prejudices – with James's Jesuit confessor providing the impetus for the plot – the allegations do appear in this case to be founded upon solid fact. Certainly, it would seem that advancing age and the repeated experience of defeat had not lessened King James's fascination with weaponry, and that he was prepared at least to consider arguments for the sudden and violent removal of his nemesis. In such a climate it is perhaps not surprising that many of his former subjects came increasingly to suspect that he was now prepared to countenance any action, however duplicitous or bloody, that would bring him closer to regaining his lost throne.

BUTLER'S TESTIMONY READS:

He went out of England about this time twelve month. He went over in the packet boat to Calais; and from thence to Dunkirk, where he met with one Mr. Thomas Moore, an old acquaintance; and stayed with him about 10 or 12 days. Among other things, Moore told the informant he had a design on foot, which if it succeeded would be a very extraordinary thing. It was the invention of [a] wind gun, that would discharge without either fire or noise. Moore promised to meet the informant at St Germains about Christmas. Accordingly, the informant went thither about the middle of November, and Moore came there a fortnight before Christmas, and brought with him the said new invented gun. Moore desired the informant to go with him to Father Sanders, King James's Confessor, which he did. Moore desired Father Sanders, to procure him an opportunity to wait upon King James and present the said gun to him; which was accordingly obtained for him, one morning early upon the Castle leeds towards the garden, nobody being permitted to come into the garden at that time. Neither did King James bring anybody with him, but the Duke of Albemarle [Henry Fitzjames, his natural son], and none being present besides but Father Sanders, Mr. Moore and the claimant. The gun was discharged and performed to admiration, whereupon King James said, 'what execution or mischief may not this engine do', to which [the] Duke of Albemarle replied: 'It may do the Prince of Orange's business', or words …

The testimony concludes:

to that effect.

The Information of William Butler.
The 11 feb: 1700¹

He went out of England about this time twelve month;
He went over in the packett boat to Calais; And
from thence to Dunkirke, where he mett with one
mr Thomas Moore, an old acquaintance; And stayd
with him about 10 or 12 days; Among other things, Moore
told the Informant he had a designe on foot, which if
it succeeded would be a very extrard thing; It was the
Invention of wind gun, that would discharge without
either fire or noise; Moor promised to meet the Informant
at St Germains about Christmas; Accordingly the
Informant went thither about the middle of November,
and Moore came there a fortnight before Christmas,
and brought him the said new Invented Gun. Moore
desired the Informant to go with him to Father
Sanders K. James Confessor, which he did; Moore desired
Father Sanders to procure him an opportunity to
wayt upon K. J. and present the said gun to him,
which was accordingly obtained for him, one morning
Early upon the Castle Leeds towards the garden, nobody
being permitted to come into the garden at that
time, neither did K. J. bring any body with him
but the D of Albemarle, and none being present
besides, but Father Saunders, mr Moore and the
Examinant. The Gun was discharged & performed
to Admiration, whereupon K. James said, what
Execution or mischief may not this Engine do, to which D. Albema
replyed; It may do the Prince of Oranges busyness or

wards

THE MAN OF SORROWS

James's last years came to be filled with religious devotions, pilgrimages, retreats and writings. In particular, his friendship with the stern and ascetic Abbe de Rancé – who presided over the Cistercian community at La Trappe – served to colour his increasingly harsh sense of his own spirituality, while the rituals of the mass and religious observance provided a structure to his day that would otherwise have been entirely lacking.

A sense of great austerity forbade the Abbe de Rancé from sitting for a formal portrait but, in 1696, he was tricked into meeting the painter, Hyacinthe Rigaud, in his cell. The artist then painted him from memory and sold copies, such as this, to the monk's many wealthy admirers.

His image as a great soldier had been left in tatters after his flight from Salisbury Plain and his defeats at the Boyne and La Hogue. It was gradually replaced by that of a priest-king, who received a divine mandate for his actions and had been made to suffer for his past transgressions and those of his rebellious subjects. James saw himself as an intermediary between God and man, who was compelled to lift the weight of sin from his former subjects and to redistribute it upon his own, increasingly bowed, shoulders (see Document 20, *James thanks God for the loss of his throne*).

It was not, therefore, the death of James II in September 1701 that excited comment from many of his contemporaries – the old King had already suffered two strokes and been ailing for some time – but rather the manner of his passing. When stripped of his finery, French courtiers noted that he looked more like a monk, with 'his beard grown long like an old Capuchin', than a king.

Yet, in an age when conduct books still flourished, the calm and collected manner in which he left the world, having first set his affairs in order and forgiven all of his enemies, was held to be the model of good behaviour. For many at St Germain, there seemed to be something that was particularly uplifting and beatific about King James's death: a last triumph after life's tragedies and repeated disappointments.

Sadly, for the peoples of Europe James's carefully orchestrated death also had far more general, and dramatic, consequences. His example had so inspired Louis XIV that he overruled the advice of his ministers and acknowledged James's young son as the rightful King of England. This act, prompted by James's dying pleas, broke the provisions of the Treaty of Ryswick and helped to pitch the Continent back into a fresh cycle of war and retribution, which beggared the French treasury and resulted in the victories of Marlborough. Without knowing it, James had passed a poisoned chalice to his heir and to his protector.

James at his religious devotions, in 1694, from a print that was once owned by Samuel Pepys. While such striking displays of personal piety did much to hearten his remaining followers, they did little to win new supporters to his flagging cause.

A prayer written by the exiled King for his private use, when his fortunes appeared to be at their lowest ebb in 1698.

James carried with him into exile an unshakeable commitment to Roman Catholicism. This commitment lay at the very core of his being and gradually began to assume the role of the connecting thread that linked together all of his past endeavours and sufferings, making them more intelligible and bearable for him. Consequently, every reverse inflicted upon the former king seemed to him to reflect the workings of a divine providence that aimed to challenge James's faith at the key junctures of his life, which could only be met and successfully surmounted

if he was able to accept the judgment of God and to work, correctly, in order to fulfil His will upon earth. James firmly believed that God had preserved him from death in battle for a purpose, but that he had sacrificed His favour and been condemned to exile on account of his enslavement to sexual desire. Thus it was imperative that James should seek to atone for his sins and to thoroughly abase himself before the Lord so that one day he might exchange his tarnished earthly crown for a heavenly one, which could never be taken from him by the hand of man.

This approach may appear somewhat curious to modern observers and some scholars have attempted to equate the

King's practice of religion with a deeper malaise, born of either physical or mental ailments. Yet this approach seeks to trivialise the nature of James's faith and to ignore its entirely rational ends: namely, as James saw it, to provide a structure, through prayer and study, to days rendered increasingly empty by his dwindling workload. It also ignores his desire to save his soul for all eternity by striving for a deeper understanding of God. As a result, he compiled lists of religious questions for discussion with his friend de Rancé, and wrote prayers and papers, containing advice for new converts and the faithful that reveal many of his innermost thoughts over the course of his latter years.

THE PRAYER READS:

I abhor and detest myself for having so often offended so gracious and merciful a God, and having lived so many years in almost a perpetual course of sin, not only in the days of my youth, when I was carried away with the heat of it, and ill example, but even after when I was come to years of more discretion, and that thou hadst been pleased to have called me from the pit of heresy, to have opened my eyes to have known and embraced thy true religion, to have …

The prayer continues:

covered my head so often in the day of battle, delivered me so many times, from the dangers of the sea, the noise of its waves, and the madness of the people, and if I had corresponded with such thy bounty hadst given me grace to endeavour to live as became a good Christian; and do give thee most humble and hearty thanks, that thou were pleased to have taken from me my three Kingdoms, by which means thou did awake me out of the lethargy of sin,

in which I had continued, I should have been forever lost, and out of thy goodness were pleased to banish me into a foreign country, where I learnt to know what was the duties, of Christianity, and endeavoured to perform them, after I had been some time in this Kingdom [i.e. France], and at La Trappe, to inspire me with such a portion of thy grace, as to endeavour to live as became a good Catholic, and as thou knowest have endeavoured to perform it, ever since …

It concludes:

my having been at that holy place, though not with that perfection as became me, and now most humbly beg of thy divine goodness, to give me grace to perform it, for thy dear son Jesus Christ's sake, who lives and reigns with thee and the Holy God, world without end, Amen. [I undertake] to repeat the seven penitential psalms, one a day, 1698.

covered my head so often in
the day of Battle, delivered
me so many tymes, from the
dangers of the Sea, the noise
of its waues, and the madnesse
of the people and given me hadst
of I hadst coorespanded with such
grace to endeauor to full
thy bounty
as became a good Christian;
and do giue thee more humble
and hearty
thankes, that thou werst pleased
to haue taken from me my
three kingdems by w: means
thou didst awake me out of the
Lethergie of sin, in w: I hadst
continued, I should haue been
for euer lost, and out of thy
goodnesse w: it pleased to ban-

bannish me into a forrain
Country, where I learnt to
know what was the dutys,
of Christionety, and endeauored to performe them after
w: such was thy goodnesse
to me, after I had been some
tyme in this kingdome, and
at La Trappe, to inspiring me
with such   endeauor to
a portion of thy
grace, as to liue as became
a good Catholike; and as
thou knewest haue endeauored
to performe it, euer since,

Who's Who

Princess Anne (1665–1714) The second daughter of James and Anne Hyde. A sickly child, she was raised as a member of the Church of England upon the express command of Charles II. She accompanied Mary of Modena to Holland in October 1678, and subsequently joined her father in exile at Brussels. Her life was immeasurably brightened by her friendship with the vivacious and strong-willed Sarah Churchill, and by her marriage to the solid and faithful Prince George of Denmark. However, she came increasingly to dislike her stepmother and feared the influence of Lord Sunderland upon her father. After her husband defected to the Prince of Orange's camp on 25 November 1688, she fled to Nottingham in the company of Bishop Compton and Lady Churchill. Her relationship with King William and Queen Mary was difficult and, at times, she appears to have considered making her peace with her exiled father. The death of the Duke of Gloucester in 1700, the last of her nineteen children, came as a terrible blow and threw the succession once more into doubt. Yet she ascended to the throne in April 1702 and quickly established herself as a diligent and genuinely popular monarch, who presided over a period of relative stability at home and military triumph abroad.

Archibald Campbell, 9th Earl of Argyll (1629–85) As a youth, he travelled through France and Germany on his 'Grand Tour', before serving as a captain in Charles II's Scottish army and fighting bravely at the Battle of Dunbar in 1650. Promoted Lieutenant-General in 1653, he attempted to reignite a Royalist revolt in the Lowlands, but laid down his arms and accepted a pardon from Cromwell in the following year. Although he welcomed the Restoration, he could do nothing to save his father from execution at the hands of a vengeful Charles II. He distinguished himself as a capable administrator and slowly rebuilt the influence of his clan, but earned the enmity of the Duke of York by his refusal, in September 1681, to swear to a new test for public office that backed James's eventual succession to the throne. Arrested and charged with treason, he mounted a daring escape attempt from Edinburgh Castle and fled to Amsterdam. Having made common cause with the Duke of Monmouth, he landed at Cariston in the Orkney Isles in May 1685, in the hope of raising a rebellion against James II. Unfortunately, poor leadership and bad communications resulted in the collapse of the rising, and he was seized on 18 June 1685. The King pressed for his death. As he had already been convicted for treason in his absence in 1681, it was judged that there was no need for a new trial. He was beheaded at the Grassmarket in Edinburgh on 30 June 1685, going to his death with calm dignity and great courage.

Colonel Joseph Bampfield (c. 1622–85) Having served in the Scottish Wars, he fought for the King in the south-west of England, before surfacing in London in 1644 as a Royalist secret agent and courier. Trusted with masterminding James's escape from the custody of Parliament, he accompanied the boy to Holland and for a time acted as his friend and mentor. However, his political ambitions were frustrated and he returned to England, where he acted as a double agent selling intelligence to both Charles II and Cromwell. In 1654 he was dismissed from the royal service and journeyed to Paris and Frankfurt as the Protector's spy. He was imprisoned following the Restoration and spent a year in the Tower. On his release in 1661, he fled to The Hague, where he eventually took service as an intelligence gatherer and military advisor. However, the rise to power of William of Orange spelled the end of his career, and he eked out his last years in poverty and ill health, publishing his autobiography in 1685 in an attempt to capitalise upon his continuing notoriety.

John Churchill, later Duke of Marlborough (1650–1720) He began his career as James's page and, through James's influence, received a commission as an ensign in the Foot Guards in 1667. He fought at the Battle of Sole Bay in 1672, and served in Flanders with the English Brigade from 1672 to 1674. Promoted Colonel of Foot in 1678, he followed James to Scotland, where he was raised to the peerage in 1682. Though he spurned James's attempts to convert him to Catholicism, he proved an able servant and an integral member of his household. He brought the news of his master's accession to Louis XIV and was raised to the English peerage in May 1685. In July 1685 he played a conspicuous part in the victory at Sedgemore and was promoted Lieutenant-General in November 1688, after Prince William's landing. He took command of the camp at Salisbury and urged James to seek a decisive battle with William's forces. Having been overruled, he fled hours later, on the night of 24 November 1688, and joined William's army at Axminster. Excoriated by James for his treachery and never completely trusted by William III, he only fully returned to prominence after the accession of Queen Anne. A string of stunning victories against the French (at Blenheim in 1704, Ramillies in 1706, Oudenarde in 1708, and Malplaquet in 1709) confirmed his reputation for military genius. But his wife's continued bullying of the Queen contributed to his tragic fall from power in 1712, which prevented the final defeat of Louis XIV.

Edward Hyde, Lord Clarendon (1609–74) A successful and wealthy lawyer, he gained the favour of Archbishop Laud and rose quickly in the royal service. Though he attacked the abuses of the monarchy in 1640, he was horrified by the radicalism of Parliament and joined the King at York in June 1642. He spent the war years in Oxford and went into exile with the Prince of Wales, beginning his seminal History of the Great Rebellion, in the Isles of Scilly, in March 1646. From the winter of 1651–2 onwards, he served as Charles II's most trusted advisor, becoming Secretary of State in 1654 and Lord

Chancellor in 1658. He was the architect of the Declaration of Breda (1660), a document that did more than any other to ensure the peaceful return of the monarchy. Hated by the King's aristocratic councillors, he was unfairly blamed for the war with the Dutch and for Charles II's childless marriage to Catherine of Braganza. After determining to cling on to office, the King, the Lords and the Commons turned against him and he fled into exile in order to avoid standing trial for his life. He died at Rouen in December 1674, but his body was permitted to be brought back for a dignified burial at Westminster Abbey a month later.

John Graham of Claverhouse (1649–89) A professional soldier, he learned his trade during the wars in Flanders from 1673–7, before returning home to Scotland. There he led his dragoons against the Covenanter rebels, earning himself a reputation as an utterly ruthless, and at times brutal, supporter of the monarchy. He was comprehensively defeated by the rebels at the Battle of Drumclog on 1 June 1679, and was lucky to escape back to Glasgow with his life. He participated in Monmouth's victory at the Battle of Bothwell Bridge on 22 June 1679, which effectively ended the rebellion, and subsequently served James loyally during his time in Scotland, rising quickly through his favour. He rode to join the royal army at Salisbury Plain in November 1688, but was devastated by its collapse and by the King's flight from London. He endeavoured to rally the Scottish Parliament for James's interest but failed. He then raised a rebellion in the Highlands in May 1689, which attempted to restore the King through force. His leadership did much to instil a common sense of purpose among the clan chiefs, but his military abilities have been consistently overemphasised on account of his heroic death at the Battle of Killiecrankie.

Edward Coleman (d. 1678) Brought up as a strict Protestant, he reacted strongly and converted to Roman Catholicism in 1670. Vain, a spendthrift and highly ambitious, he served as secretary to both James and Mary of Modena. At court he acted as a proselytiser for his faith and conducted a secret correspondence with the Papal Nuncio in Brussels and the French Court that, once revealed, resulted in his conviction for treason and swift execution.

Louis II, Prince de Condé (1621–86) One of the foremost soldiers of his age, Condé was given the independent command of an army at just 22 years of age. At the Battle of Rocroi in May 1643, he shattered a veteran Spanish army and gained for France her greatest military victory in a hundred years. Though further successes followed in the Rhineland and Catalonia, his high birth and enormous military prestige created jealousy among the other princes, and he came to be seen as harbouring designs upon the French throne. Having gone unrewarded for his part in saving the French monarchy in 1649, he went into rebellion against it. Now allied with Spain, he was defeated by Turenne outside Paris and again at the Battle of the Dunes. However, he obtained an amnesty after peace was declared in 1659 and was reconciled to Louis XIV. Thereafter, he faithfully served the French crown, distinguishing himself as a brave and, at times, brilliant tactician in campaigns against the Dutch and the Holy Roman Empire. Though dogged by ill health, he remained a respected member of Louis XIV's court and died peacefully in his bed at the Palace of Fontainebleau.

Thomas Osborne, Earl of Danby (1631–1712) Raised as a strong Royalist, he spent part of his youth in Paris, before taking his seat in the Commons in 1665 as MP for York. He led the attacks on Clarendon in 1667 that brought about his fall, but thereafter was promoted through royal favour. Eloquent, able and good-looking, he rose through the Treasury Office to become Charles II's first minister in 1673. He promoted the marriage of Princess Mary and William of Orange, but was brought down by the outbreak of the Popish Plot in December

1678. Discredited and unpopular, he spent the next five years in the Tower, but was never brought to trial. Freed in 1684, he quickly asserted himself as an active and powerful member of the Tory Party, but within a year of James II's accession he found himself in opposition to the Crown on account of his religious principles. He signed the invitation for William of Orange to come to England in June 1688, and seized York in his name in November, raising the North in rebellion. During the Convention Parliament, he argued that James II had left the throne vacant and sat as President of the Council in February 1690, effectively serving as William's first minister. Though created Marquis of Carmarthen, he was not restored to his power base in the Treasury, as he had wished, and was seriously damaged by allegations of corruption in 1695. He left office in May 1699, and spent his retirement attempting to defend his conduct during Charles II's reign. Though he was still considered as a candidate for the post of Lord Privy Seal in 1711, his latter years were marred by poor health and an eventual decline into senility.

Anthony Farmer (1658–after 1687) As a young man he attended Cambridge University, but was more distinguished for his scandalous conduct and quarrelsome nature than for the rigour of his studies. After teaching at a non-conformist school in Wiltshire, he joined Magdalen Hall, Oxford, but he soon rowed with the Fellows and was forced out and into Magdalen College. However, his fortunes took a turn for the better when he converted to Roman Catholicism at the beginning of 1687 and gained the favour of the King. In spite of the controversy that surrounded him, and the frequent reports of his drunkenness, James backed his candidature for the presidency of the college in April 1687. However, after a storm of protest greeted his nomination, Judge Jeffreys cross-examined him on 29 July 1687, and found the allegations made against him to be true. On 14 August James switched his support to Samuel Parker, Bishop of Oxford, and Farmer fell back into the obscurity from which he came.

Henri de Duras, Earl of Feversham (c. 1640–1709) A nephew of Marshal Turenne, he chose a military career and sought preferment under James. He became a naturalised Englishman in 1665 and, in the same year, distinguished himself at the Battle of Lowestoft. However, he was hit in the head by falling timbers when a fire ravaged Temple Lane in January 1679, and was seriously injured. He never fully recovered his former quickness of thought and action. Despite his strong Protestantism, he was devoted to James and joined the Privy Council upon his accession in 1685. In July 1685 he was victorious at the Battle of Sedgemore but was heavily criticised for his belated arrival upon the field. This did not prevent his promotion to Commander-in-Chief of the English Army in 1686. He oversaw the disbandment of his forces in December 1688, and was relieved of his military commands at the Glorious Revolution. He successfully fought attempts to banish him to Holland when a French invasion threatened in May 1692, and was finally laid to rest in the Huguenot Chapel in the Strand.

Sir Edmund Berry Godfrey (1621–78) A wealthy entrepreneur who made his fortune in the wood trade, he rose to become Justice of the Peace for Westminster. He refused to flee from London at the height of the Plague in 1665, and helped to give charity to the sick and the poor. He clashed with the Court in 1669 after attempting to collect a debt from the King's physician, but remained an extremely well-liked figure in the City. His mysterious death, therefore, proved all the more shocking. An inquest returned a verdict of wilful murder, though it was rumoured, both at the time and since, that he had actually committed suicide and that his family had moved his body in an attempt to preserve his reputation.

Henrietta Maria, Queen of England (1609–69) A French princess and the wife of Charles I, she was the mother of Charles II and James II. Pleasure seeking, extravagant and staunchly Catholic, she was unpopular with her subjects and did not enjoy good or close relationships with her children. She sought refuge in France in July 1644 and, following the execution of her husband in 1649, lost the remnants of her political influence. She vehemently opposed James's marriage to Anne Hyde in 1660, and her return to England after the Restoration was neither happy nor rewarding. She finally returned to France in 1665, settling at Colombes outside Paris, where she died.

Anne Hyde, Duchess of York (1637–71) Accompanied her mother and siblings into exile in 1649, she became a Maid of Honour to the Princess of Orange in 1654. Intelligent and vivacious, she quickly became a favourite within the royal household and accompanied the Princess on a visit to Paris in 1656 to visit Henrietta Maria. On the journey, she met James and, in November 1659, he promised her marriage. Despite her father's furious opposition, she secured the backing of the King and was married to James in 1660. She was to bear him eight children, though only two daughters – the Princesses Mary and Anne – survived into adulthood. She exerted an enormous influence on her husband, but was quick to make enemies as well as friends. In order to counter-act James's numerous infidelities, she took Henry Sidney as her lover and made sure that her husband's mistress, Lady Chesterfield, was banished from court. She converted to Roman Catholicism through the influence of Father Hunt, a Franciscan, and – having contracted breast cancer – died proclaiming her faith.

James Francis Edward, the 'Old Pretender' (1688–1766) Spirited away to France by his mother in December 1688, he was raised in the gloomy and intellectually arid climate of the exiled court at St Germain. Proclaimed king with French approval after the death of his father, he mounted an abortive attempt to land in Scotland in 1705, and fought for Louis XIV at the battles of Oudenarde in 1708 and Malplaquet in 1709. Forced out of France by the Peace Treaty of 1713, he reached Scotland during the rising of 1715, but showed little leadership or judgement and hurried back to the Continent in February 1716. He retired to Rome in 1719 and, though the lives of his two sons kept Jacobite hopes alive, he provided an increasingly awkward and melancholic figurehead for the movement. It was left to King George III to pay for his monument in St Peter's, Rome, in 1819.

Judge George Jeffreys (1648–89) As ambitious as he was unprincipled, Jeffreys possessed scant legal training but had a real talent for cross-examining witnesses and detecting flaws in their testimony. He came to prominence as a City of London lawyer before being appointed as James's Solicitor General in 1677. He took part in the trials of those implicated in the Popish Plot, before acting as an instrument of royal power in breaking the City of London's Charter in 1681, prosecuting radicals after the failure of the Oxford Parliament and the Rye House Plot, and extending James's influence in the Post Office and East India Company. He condemned Algernon Sidney to death in 1683, and earned lasting infamy for his brutal sentencing of prisoners after the collapse of Monmouth's rebellion in 1685. In November 1688 he was one of the five lords who sat on the Council of State after the King left to join the army at Salisbury. He surrendered the Great Seal to James on the night of 8 December 1688, but was shocked by the King's refusal to make any provision for his own escape. Universally hated, he was confined to the Tower and died there before he could be brought to proper account.

William Laud, Archbishop of Canterbury (1573–1645) Authoritarian, impatient of doctrinal controversy and desirous of social order, this son of a Reading clothier enjoyed a meteoric career in the Church of England, becoming the Bishop of St David's in 1621 and the Bishop of London in 1628. In 1633 Charles I appointed him Archbishop of Canterbury. However, his drive to centralise Church government, reinject an element of splendour back into the Anglican

service and press for harsh sentences for his critics went against the spirit of, and ultimately fractured, the religious settlement established in England during the reigns of Elizabeth I and James I. Identified by his Parliamentary foes as the source of the afflictions in both Church and State, he was impeached in March 1641 and sent to the Tower. Tried for treason three years later, he was executed on 10 January 1645.

Mary II (1662–94) The eldest surviving child of James and Anne Hyde, she was doted upon as an infant. Raised as a member of the Church of England, she grew into a deeply religious but cheerful and intelligent young woman. She was married to William of Orange in 1677 and returned to England in February 1689, when she and her husband were offered the Crown as joint sovereigns. Tragically, she was struck down by smallpox and died in December 1694. She was deeply mourned in England, but James drew censure by refusing to put his court into mourning on his daughter's passing.

Mary of Modena (1658–1718) Brought up as a strict Roman Catholic, she reluctantly submitted to her marriage to James in 1673, but their relationship came to be marked by a deep and lasting affection. Crowned Queen in April 1685, she made a pilgrimage to St Winfred's Well in Wales in August 1687 to pray for a healthy son. Her appeals were seemingly answered and, in June 1688, she gave birth to James Francis Edward amid a climate of general suspicion and widespread disbelief. In December 1688 she fled to France, together with her son, and took up residence at St Germain-en-Laye. Following her husband's death, she stood as regent for the boy and did much to shape the Jacobite movement, and to perpetuate James II's memory. Her years in exile were characterised by religious devotion and her patronage of the convent of La Chaillot outside Paris.

Princess Mary of Orange (1631–60) A pawn in the dynastic alliances of the House of Stuart, she was married to the 14-year-old Prince William II of Orange in May 1641, but was permitted to remain in England until her twelfth year. She travelled to Holland with her mother in February 1642 and, once her husband had come to power in 1647, she used her position to sustain the flagging Royalist cause and welcomed many exiles to her court. However, her husband died suddenly in November 1650, and her influence was eroded by the States General. Her only child, William, was thus born eight days after his father's death. Mary visited her brothers at Whitehall in September 1660, but was struck down by the smallpox epidemic that raged there in December. She died after five days of sickness on 24 December, refusing to see her mother or listen to her injunctions that she convert to Catholicism. She was buried in Westminster Abbey.

John Drummond, Earl and titular Duke of Melfort, (1649–1714) James's loyal client, he became Lieutenant-General and Master of Ordinance in Scotland in 1680, then deputy treasurer of that kingdom a year later. In 1684 he was appointed Secretary of State for Scotland and, helped by his timely conversion to Roman Catholicism, he effectively ruled Scotland, alongside his elder brother, for the next three years. He fled to France in December 1688, and the Edinburgh mob vented their frustration by sacking his home. He accompanied James to Ireland in 1689, but his arrogance and appalling lack of tact led him to be sent away, on a mission to Rome. Back at St Germain by late 1691, his ascendancy was brought to an end by the arrival of his rival, Middleton. By 1696 he had been denied permission, by James, to return to England. However, the King forgave him on his deathbed, and he eked out his remaining years at Angers in relative comfort and ease.

Charles Middleton, 2nd Earl of Middleton, (c. 1640–1719) Having accompanied James back to Edinburgh in 1682, he was appointed to the Scottish Privy Council. In 1684 he joined the English Privy Council and, after James's accession, managed the House of Commons

for the King. In 1688 he remained loyal to James and was imprisoned in the Tower in May 1692, when a French invasion was feared. In July 1694 he joined the exiled court at St Germain and quickly displaced Melfort as its first minister. He converted to Roman Catholicism after James II's deathbed injunction, and was the architect of the abortive Jacobite expedition to Scotland in 1707. In December 1713 he resigned as Jacobite Secretary of State and returned to St Germain, where he served Mary of Modena as her Great Chamberlain until her death.

James Scott, Duke of Monmouth (1649–85) The illegitimate child of Charles II and Lucy Walters, he was born in Rotterdam and raised in Paris, before being summoned to the English court in 1662. Indulged by Charles II, it was rumoured that he would be recognised by the King as his legitimate heir. This was enough to raise the suspicions of the Duke of York, and his jealousy was compounded by Monmouth's acceptance of the post of Captain-General in 1670. In 1672 Monmouth led the English Brigade in Flanders and won fame for his bravery at the siege of Maastricht in 1673. He ended the Covenanter rebellion at the Battle of Bothwell Bridge in 1678, but his ambition led him into opposition as he moulded himself as the champion of Protestant rights and as a rival to James in the succession to the throne. Stripped of his commands, he made common cause with Shaftesbury but was implicated in the Rye House Plot to assassinate the King in 1683, and fled to the Continent. The death of Charles II in 1685 destroyed any chance of a reconciliation between father and son. Monmouth's subsequent attempt to seize the throne resulted in defeat at Sedgemore and swift capture. His execution on 15 July 1685 was hideously bungled, but he displayed courage and much fortitude in the face of the headsman's gross incompetence.

Algernon Percy, Earl of Northumberland (1602–68) This proud and dignified northern magnate travelled widely in Europe before being appointed by Charles I as the Admiral of the Fleet in 1636. Though he disapproved of the King's policies towards the Scots, he still did much to organise the war effort against them. However, ill health prevented him from taking command of the Royal Army in August 1640. He was dismissed as Lord Admiral in June 1642 and gave his support to the Parliamentary cause. He was uncomfortable in his role as Governor to the King's captive children and, in 1649, opposed the trial of Charles I. Thereafter, he dropped out of public life and, though he supported the Restoration in 1660, he wished to see Charles II return upon binding terms. In that year, he became a Privy Councillor but was effectively marginalised and exercised no further influence on the formulation of government policy.

Titus Oates (1649–1705) A notorious perjurer, his expulsion from school did not prevent him from entering the Anglican clergy. In April 1677 he converted to Roman Catholicism and entered the English College at Valladolid two months later. Having been quickly expelled, he joined the English College at St Omer in December 1677, but was once again expelled for gross misconduct in June 1678. By September 1678 he was circulating stories of a Popish Plot that aimed to assassinate the King and forcibly re-convert the English people, with the help of foreign armies. Amid the subsequent public hysteria, he testified against 35 individuals who went to their deaths on trumped-up charges of treason. However, he over-reached himself in May 1684, when he called the Duke of York a traitor. Arrested at a London coffee house, he was jailed and sentenced to be fined and severely flogged after James's accession. The King probably intended the blows to kill him, but he survived. Having run through his wife's fortune, he quickly fell into debt and was turned out of a Baptist community in Wapping in 1701 as a hypocrite and liar. It would seem that only death could bring an end to his spinning of deceit and silence his continually wagging tongue.

Richard Graham, Viscount Preston (1648–95) A Tory and High Anglican, he marshalled votes for James in his Parliament of 1685 and was admitted to the Privy Council in October of that year. After the dismissal of Sunderland, he became Lord President of the Privy Council and, in November 1688, was one of the committee of five lords who governed the capital during James's absence. He attempted to rally support for the exiled King among Protestant peers and churchmen, but he was captured carrying incriminating correspondence over to James on New Year's Day, 1690. Having given evidence against his fellow conspirators, he saved his life but sacrificed his reputation and retired to a cheerless obscurity on his estates.

Abbé Armand Jean de Rancé (1626–1700) James's spiritual mentor had re-established the rule of St Benedict, in its most severe form, at the Abbey of La Trappe in the early 1660s. Private study was discontinued in favour of hard manual work, while food was rationed to a bare minimum and a strict vow of silence was observed. James first made the Abbé's acquaintance after his return from Ireland in 1690 and thereafter sought to go on annual retreats to the monastery, while maintaining a regular correspondence with de Rancé. Though the nomination of Abbé's successor proved extremely acrimonious and threatened to destroy de Rancé's reforms, James's faith in his friend remained largely unshaken and he was greatly saddened by his death.

Lawrence Hyde, Earl of Rochester (1641–1711) The second son of Lord Clarendon and brother of Anne Hyde, he defended his father against impeachment charges in 1667 and distinguished himself as an able young MP for Newport, Cornwall. He served as ambassador to Poland in 1676 and fought against the plans to exclude James from the throne on account of his religion. He masterminded the Tory reaction of the last years of Charles II's reign and was made Lord President of the Council in 1684. He became Lord Treasurer on the accession of

James II but found himself consistently under-mined by Sunderland and opposed by Mary of Modena and the Jesuits at court. Having refused to convert to Catholicism, he was dismissed from office on 10 December 1685 and retired into private life. In November 1688 he argued that James should call a free Parliament and negotiate with William of Orange, but the King chose not to listen to him until it was too late. He opposed offering the Crown to William and Mary but pragmatically agreed to swearing allegiance to them in March 1689. Three years later, he took his seat once more upon the Privy Council and enjoyed considerable influence due to his relationship with his niece, Queen Mary. He served as Lord Lieutenant of Ireland from 1700 to 1703 but was dismissed after antagonis-ing the Duke of Marlborough. In 1710 he became Lord President of the Council. He died suddenly, on the night of 1–2 May 1711, at his house in Whitehall.

Anthony Ashley Cooper, Earl of Shaftesbury (1621–83) This able and highly intelligent statesman came to prominence, after deserting from the Royalists to Parliament, in the service of the English Republic. However, he welcomed the Restoration and, in 1661, was raised to the peerage. He took an active role in the Commit-tee for Trade and Plantations and in 1669 over-saw the drawing-up of a progressive constitution for Carolina by his servant, John Locke, that en-shrined the principle of religious toleration. He became Lord Chancellor in 1672 and backed the resumption of war against the Dutch. However, he forfeited the King's favour through his will-ingness to use the provisions of the Test Act to rid himself of his Roman Catholic rivals for high office. Having opposed James's remarriage, he was dismissed from his post as Chancellor in late 1673 and from his place on the Privy Council in May 1674. He quickly established himself as the leading critic of growing royal power. He pressed for James's exclusion from the throne and created the nucleus of a party machine about him in Parliament, but was twice outmanoeuvred by Charles II. He grasped at a return to office as President of the Privy Council in April 1679, but was wrong-footed by the sudden prorogation of Parliament and by his sudden dismissal from office in October. Similarly, at the Oxford Parlia-ment in January 1681, he and his Whig support-ers faltered before a carefully choreographed display of royal power. Though he was acquitted by a London jury of a charge of treason and fled into exile in Holland, his health was broken and he died shortly afterwards. His most durable and fitting tribute remains the Habeas Corpus Act, which he forced on to the statute books, against royal opposition, in 1679.

Algernon Sidney (1622–83) The son of the Earl of Leicester, he served in Ireland before being wounded in 1644 fighting for Parliament at the Battle of Marston Moor. Commissioned as a Colonel in the New Model Army in 1645, he was promoted to Lieutenant-General and served in the Irish campaign of 1647. He sat on the Council of State in 1652 but broke with Cromwell over the suppression of that body and the watering down of the Republic. Returning to govern on the Council of State in 1659, when the Commonwealth was briefly re-established, he was on a diplomatic mission to the Continent at the Restoration and wisely chose to remain in exile. He travelled widely, attempting unsuccess-fully to rally support for the Republican cause. In 1677 he returned to England in order to settle his family's affairs. Caught up in the whirlwind of the Tory reaction, he was arrested in July 1683 for complicity in the Rye House Plot. Though taunted by Judge Jeffreys, he defended himself ably and went to his death on Tower Hill with enormous courage, proudly proclaiming his dedication to the 'Good old cause' of Republi-canism that had sustained him since his youth.

Henri de la Tour d'Auvergne, Vicomte Turenne (1611–75) The son of the Prince of Sedan, Turenne saw service in the Dutch army before offering his sword to France. He led the French army into Germany in the latter stages of the Thirty Years' War. Following his victory at the Battle of Zusmarshausen in 1648, the Emperor was forced to sue for peace and the devastating conflict was brought to an end. Faced by Condé's rebellion, Turenne effectively saved the French monarchy and finally triumphed over the Spanish and their allies at the Battle of the Dunes in 1658. He became Marshal-General in 1660 and masterminded Louis XIV's campaigns against the Dutch Republic in 1667–8 and 1672. Having protected Alsace from invasion by the Emperor and the German princes in 1674, he broke his enemies at the Battle of Turckheim in January 1675, ensuring France's hold on the province. However, he was killed while out on reconnaissance before the Battle of Sasbach in July 1675.

Richard Talbot, Earl of Tyrconnel (1630–91)

The champion of the Irish Catholic community, Talbot's early life was shaped by almost constant warfare. He served with Ormonde's army before being wounded and left for dead at the fall of Drogheda in 1649. Having escaped from Ireland, he settled in Madrid in 1653, before being brought to the attention of James as a man of action who was prepared to undertake the assassination of Oliver Cromwell. He served alongside James during his campaigns in Flanders and was at the Battle of the Dunes in 1658. At the Restoration, he was appointed a Gentleman of the Duke of York's Bedchamber but was soon in trouble with the authorities for duelling. In 1661 he was sent to the Tower, on the first of two occasions, for threatening violence to Lord Ormonde, the Viceroy of Ireland. He fought at the Battle of Lowestoft in 1665 and was captured by the Dutch at the Battle of Sole Bay in 1672. Though he was arrested in Ireland in 1678 on suspicion of involvement in the Popish Plot, his career flourished as the Tory reaction took hold and James

ascended the throne. In 1686 he was appointed Lord-Lieutenant of the Irish army and began to swell its numbers, while purging its officer corps of Protestants. In January 1687 he became Viceroy of Ireland and loyally held the country for James in the winter of 1688–9. Although his wise advice to James in 1690, to avoid a direct confrontation with William III, was overruled, he fought bravely at the Boyne and kept Jacobite resistance alive in Ireland long after his master had fled back to France. Prematurely aged and worn out by his labours, as well as by his equally active pursuit of pleasure, he died in August 1691 and was buried in Limerick Cathedral.

William III, Prince of Orange and King of Great Britain and Ireland (1650–1702)

The only child of William II of Orange and Princess Mary Stuart, he devoted himself to rebuilding the shattered fortunes of his House and to saving the United Provinces from being over-whelmed by French military might. In 1672 he was appointed Captain-General of the United Provinces and managed to save the Dutch Republic from destruction by breaking the dykes and flooding the route of the French advance. Having made a favourable impression upon English political opinion, he married James's eldest daughter, Mary, in 1677, and established himself as a future candidate for the throne. Weaving together a series of European alliances aimed at limiting French power, he was dismayed by James's catholicising policies and feared that he might ultimately seek to ally himself with Louis XIV. The birth of James Francis Edward threatened his own succession. Seizing his chance, he launched a pre-emptive invasion of England in November 1688, which aimed to wring a series of concessions from his uncle and father-in-law. The total collapse of James's regime and the King's flight unexpectedly handed him the crown, though he was forced by Parliament to rule jointly with his wife. He defeated James at the Battle of the Boyne in 1690 and subsequently fought Louis XIV's armies to a bloody stalemate in Flanders.

Chronology

1633	14 October Birth of James at St James's Palace, London.
1642	23 April James is held captive in Hull. He is released after several hours.
	23 October The Battle of Edgehill.
	29 October James enters Oxford at his father's side. He will spend most of the next three-and-a-half years there.
1645	14 June The Battle of Naseby.
1646	20 June Surrender of Oxford. James becomes a prisoner of Parliament.
1648	21–22 April James escapes from the Earl of Northumberland's custody at St James's Palace, and sails for Holland.
1649	30 January Execution of Charles I.
1649–50	James on the island of Jersey.
1651	August Rebellion of the Prince de Condé. Outbreak of the Second Fronde in France.
1652	May The siege of Étampes.
	June Fights at the Battle of the Faubourg Saint-Antoine, outside Paris.
	December James leads an attempt to storm Ligny Castle. The stronghold surrenders next day.
1653	September James at the siege of Mousson.
1654	Spring Promoted to Lieutenant-General.
	August Fights the Spanish before their lines at Arras. Turenne breaks the siege and relieves the stricken city.
1655	September James leads a great foraging party into the countryside about Chievres.
	October Peace treaty between France and England.
	November James is forced to leave the French army.
1656	February Meets Anne Hyde on the road between Peronne and Cambrai.
1657	May James joins the Spanish army at Mons.
	September Takes part in an abortive attack on the fort at Mardyck.
1658	14/24 June The Battle of the Dunes.
	3 September Death of Oliver Cromwell, Lord Protector of England.
1660	January James becomes High Admiral of Spain. General Monck leads his army back from Scotland across the Coldstream, and into England.
	16 May James is confirmed in his position as Lord High Admiral of England by Charles II.
	29 May Charles II enters London in triumph.
	5 September James marries Anne Hyde.
1664	July James becomes Governor of the Royal Adventurers' Company trading into Africa.
	August The city and colony of New Amsterdam are seized by an English expeditionary force and renamed in James's honour as New York.
1665	4 March War declared upon Holland.
	3 June The Battle of Lowestoft.
	July–November Serious outbreak of the plague.
	August–September James moves his household to York.

1666	2–6 September The Great Fire of London.
1667	7–14 June The Dutch attack the royal dockyards and carry off the flagship of the English fleet.
	21 July A peace treaty is signed between England and Holland at Breda.
	30 August Clarendon is stripped of his offices.
	29 November Clarendon escapes to France, to avoid standing trial for his life.
1668–9	Winter James begins to have religious doubts.
1669	January James decides to convert to Roman Catholicism.
1670	22 May Secret Treaty of Dover signed.
1671	31 March Death of Anne Hyde, Duchess of York.
1672	17 March Charles II declares war on Holland, once more.
	28 May The Battle of Sole Bay.
1673	29 March Passage of the First Test Act.
	15 June James is forced to give up his commands as Lord High Admiral, Governor of Portsmouth and Warden of the Cinque Ports.
	30 September James is married to Mary of Modena by proxy.
	21 November Mary of Modena lands at Dover and is married to James according to Anglican rites.
1674	9 February Peace signed with Holland.
1677	4 November James's eldest daughter, Mary, marries Prince William of Orange.
1678	August The allegations of a 'Popish Plot' first surface.
	12 October Discovery of the body of Magistrate Godfrey.
	3 December Execution of Edward Coleman.
1679	3 March James leaves for exile in Brussels.
	21 May The Exclusion Bill receives a second parliamentary reading.
	27 May Parliament is prorogued, effectively killing the Exclusion Bill.
	29 August On hearing of Charles II's illness, James starts back for England.
	24 November James arrives in Edinburgh.
1680	2–11 November Second Exclusion Bill introduced and passed in the Commons.
	15 November The Bill is defeated in the House of Lords.
1681	21–28 March The Oxford Parliament.
	28 July James opens the Scottish Parliament.
1682	8 April James is welcomed back to London by Tory crowds.
1683	January James becomes Governor of the Hudson's Bay Company.
1684	May James returns to his office as Lord High Admiral and once again sits on the Privy Council, in clear defiance of the Test Acts.
1685	6 February Death of Charles II.
	23 April James II is crowned King at Westminster Abbey on St George's Day.
	19 May New Parliament meets.
	11 June Monmouth lands at Lyme and raises a rebellion against James in the West Country.
	17 June Capture of the Earl of Argyll.

1685	6 July The Battle of Sedgemoor.
	August–September The Bloody Assizes.
	10/22 October Louis XIV revokes the Edict of Nantes.
	20 November James prorogues his first, and only, Parliament.
1686	June Goddens *vs.* Hales court case.
	July Commissioners for Ecclesiastical Causes appointed.
	September Bishop Compton of London is suspended.
1687	4 April First Declaration of Indulgence.
	August–September James embarks upon an 'election tour' of Wales, the west and the Midlands.
1688	27 April Second Declaration of Indulgence.
	10 June Birth of the Prince of Wales.
	30 June Acquittal of the Seven Bishops. Seven magnates sign a letter inviting William of Orange to come to England.
	5 November William of Orange lands at Torbay.
	19 November James joins his army on Salisbury Plain.
	24 November James leaves the camp at Salisbury and orders the army to retreat.
	12 December James flees Whitehall in the early hours. He is captured by Kentish fishermen.
	23 December James slips away from Rochester, and takes passage for France.
1689	6 February Parliament declares the Crown to be vacant and offers it to William and Mary.
	24 March James enters Dublin.
	11 April William and Mary are crowned joint monarchs.
	17 April James delivers a summons for the surrender of Derry. It is refused.
	27 July The Battle of Killiecrankie.
	28 July The blockade of Derry is broken. The Jacobite army abandons the siege and retreats three days later.
	21 August The Battle of Dunkeld.
1690	14 June William III lands in Ireland.
	1 July The Battle of the Boyne.
	4 July James takes ship back to France.
1692	23–24 May/3–4 June The Battle of La Hogue.
1694	28 December Queen Mary dies.
1696	March Failure of the Assassination Plot.
	April James's invasion force is stood down on the Normandy coast. He returns dejectedly to St Germain.
	June–September James is suggested as a candidate for the throne of Poland, but he refuses to be considered.
1697	10/20 September The Peace of Ryswick is signed.
1701	5/16 September Death of James II at St Germain-en-Laye.

Further Reading

Philip Aubrey, *The Defeat of James Stuart's Armada, 1692* (Leicester University Press, 1979). An excellent monograph detailing the struggle for naval supremacy between England, Holland and France in the closing years of the seventeenth century, and charting the series of military defeats that culminated in the failure of James II to be restored to his thrones.

Stephen B. Baxter, *William III* (Longmans, 1966). Still the standard account of the life of the King and Stadholder, vibrantly written and exceptionally well researched from both the English and Dutch archives.

Hillaire Belloc, *James the Second* (Faber & Gwyer, 1928). Though often inaccurate in its details, this passionate and polemical attempt to rehabilitate the reputation of James II was deeply influential for many subsequent right-wing writers, both scholarly and popular, who attempted to take the 'Glory' out of the Revolution of 1688–9.

Bishop Gilbert Burnet, *History of His Own Time*, ed. M. J. Routh (6 vols, Georg Olms, 1969). A major primary source for the period, written by one of the expedition that accompanied William to England. As one would expect, it reflects the preferences of its author, a Scottish Whig, but is still the single most perceptive and important memoir of the Glorious Revolution and Britain in the 1690s.

John Callow, *The Making of King James II* (Sutton, 2000). A study of James's youth, early manhood and military career; it demonstrates the manner in which he sought to first fashion and then project an inflated self-image as a warrior, imperialist and general of great distinction.

John Callow, *The King in Exile. James II: Warrior, King, and Saint, 1689–1701* (Sutton, 2004). Historians have largely ignored James's fate as a king without a crown. This book sheds new light on the last twelve years of his life, from his disastrous intervention in Irish politics and his defeat at the Boyne, to his gradual acceptance of his role as the client of the King of France and his quest for personal salvation.

Winston Spencer Churchill, *Marlborough: His Life and Times* (Book One, University of Chicago Press, rpr. 2002) A stunning biography chronicling Marlborough's early service in James's household. Deeply partisan and sometimes highly selective, but written with verve and a mastery of the English language that is still unsurpassed.

James Stanier Clarke, *The Life of James the Second, King of England, collected out of Memoirs writ of his own Hand* (2 vols, Longman, 1816). Comprising in part memoirs dictated personally by James II and in part other explanatory texts woven together by his editors in the early years of the eighteenth century, this was the supreme propaganda work produced by the Jacobite court in exile. This is how James II wanted to be remembered by posterity and, though its claims should be treated with caution, it has been an invaluable source for every one of his subsequent biographers.

Ronald Hutton, *Charles II* (Clarendon Press, 1989). The definitive biography of the king, brilliantly written and superbly researched, which strips away the veneer of myth from the "Merry Monarch" to reveal the ruthless and capable politician that lurked beneath.

J. R. Jones, *The Revolution of 1688 in England* (Weidenfeld and Nicolson, 1972). The first and arguably the greatest of the revisionist accounts of the Glorious Revolution, well researched and painting a compelling portrait of James's policies, the book stresses their coherence and their reasonable chances of success, had it not been for the decisive intervention of William of Orange.

Robert Latham and William Mathews (eds), *The Diary of Samuel Pepys* (10 vols, Harper Collins, 1970-83). As fresh, as lively and as thoroughly revealing today as when its entries were first written. A treasure and a delight for both the interested reader and the hardened historian.

Thomas Babbington Macaulay, *The History of England: From the Accession of James the Second* (6 vols, Macmillan, 1913–15). Beautifully written, deeply dramatic and thoroughly opinionated, this was for many years the standard account of James's fall. Though many of its conclusions have since been challenged, it remains the classic Whig account of the Glorious Revolution and a model of narrative history that has been much imitated but never equalled.

John Miller, *James II* (2nd edition, Yale University Press, 2000). A major contribution to our knowledge of the king that is both scholarly and judicious, and based upon s ources that were simply unavailable to Turner a generation before.

Michael Mullett, *James II and English Politics, 1678–1688* (Routledge, 1994). The best brief introduction to James's reign and the anti-Catholic hysteria that threatened to engulf his fortunes at every turn. An elegant, clear and thorough exposition of a political system that is at first sight, very different from our own.

A. Lytton Sells, *The Memoirs of James II: His Campaigns as Duke of York* (Chatto & Windus, 1962). A splendid modern edition of James's gripping and evocative tales of warfare in France and Flanders during the 1650s.

John Gerald Simms, *Jacobite Ireland, 1685–91* (Routledge & Kegan Paul, 1969). A balanced, clear and comprehensive account of the Jacobite wars in Ireland that is both readable, fascinating and the last word on a subject that continues to evoke the fiercest of sectarian passions.

F. C. Turner, *James II* (Eyre & Spottiswoode, 1948). The seminal single-volume life of the King, meticulously researched, tightly written and utterly compelling in its vision of the gradual erosion of James's spirit and his political effectiveness.

Picture Credits

Index